59 Goytisolo: Campos de Níjar

Critical Guides to Spanish Texts

EDITED BY JOHN VAREY, ALAN DEYERMOND, & CATHERINE DAVIES

GOYTISOLO

CAMPOS DE NÍJAR

Abigail Lee Six

Lecturer of Spanish
Queen Mary and Westfield College, London

Grant & Cutler Ltd
1996

ISBN 0 7293 0379 9

DEPÓSITO LEGAL: V. 4.894 - 1995

Printed in Spain by
Artes Gráficas Soler, S.A., Valencia
for GRANT & CUTLER LTD
55–57 GREAT MARLBOROUGH STREET, LONDON W1V 2AY

Contents

Contents

Prefatory Note

References to the text of *Campos de Níjar* are twofold: first, to the Biblioteca de Bolsillo edition (Barcelona: Seix Barral, 1983), and, second, to that in the series of the Tamesis Texts (London: Tamesis Texts, 1984). References to *La Chanca* are to the Biblioteca Breve 5th edition (Barcelona: Seix Barral, 1987).

The figures in parentheses in italic type refer to the numbered items in the Bibliographical Note; where appropriate, these are followed by page numbers.

I should like to express my gratitude to my colleagues, the editors of this series, Professors A.D. Deyermond and J.E. Varey, for their constructive comments and guidance.

[Handwritten annotations at top: "social realist period (50's) → experimental phase (66)" with arrows pointing to "CAMPOS = TRANS."]

1. Introduction

Campos de Níjar, published in 1960, was the first of Juan Goytisolo's three travel books; it was followed in 1962 by *La Chanca*, also about southern Spain, and in the same year, by *Pueblo en marcha*, a polemical eulogy of post-revolutionary Cuba. These works thus appear in comparatively rapid succession, and do so at an important juncture in the author's literary evolution, for they carry him over from the social-realist period of his 1950s novels to the experimental phase that was heralded by *Señas de identidad* in 1966. David Henn has shown how 'they reveal important thematic links' between the two periods (*6*, p.256); but for present purposes, suffice it to say that we may expect to find the ambivalence of a transitional period in *Campos*. First, there is fluctuation between the attempt at objectivity of the early works and the highly — and latterly, exuberantly — subjective narrative stance of the mature fiction. Goytisolo has testified to this change of approach in an interview:

> Si me propongo describir la realidad de un barrio pobre de Barcelona o del sur de España, yo no puedo escribir como si fuese un murciano que vive en las chabolas de Barcelona, un campesino pobre de Níjar o un pescador de La Chanca. Cuando me introduzco en su mundo, para mí extraño, para mí chocante, no puedo renunciar a llevar conmigo una tradición cultural, un medio social, una educación. Si hago un análisis de este mundo, ya sea de una región pobre del sur o de Barcelona, estoy obligado a hacerlo desde mi propio enfoque, desde mi propio punto de vista. [...] A partir de *La resaca* [written immediately before *Campos* and from the point of view of a southern immigrant in Catalonia] me di

cuenta que, si me proponía reflejar una serie de
fenómenos propios de la sociedad española, tenía que
[...] aceptar el subjetivismo.[1]

But in a second respect too, *Campos* was a turning-point. This is
how Goytisolo puts it in his autobiography, and the passage is worth
quoting at some length, for it also acts as a warning to insouciant
readers to keep their wits about them when first approaching the
work:

La composición de *Campos de Níjar* cierra un capítulo
de mi narrativa en relación con España. Escrito con un
cuidado extremo, a fin de sortear los escollos de la
censura, es un libro cuya técnica, estructura y enfoque se
explican ante todo en función de aquélla: empleo de
elipsis, asociaciones de ideas, deducciones implícitas
que si resultan oscuras a un público habituado a
manifestarse libremente no lo son para quienes,
sometidos largo tiempo a los grillos de una censura
férrea, adquieren, como observara agudamente Blanco
White,[2] 'la viveza de los mudos para entenderse por
señas'. [...] Aunque esto constituía un triunfo del que
entonces me sentí orgulloso, una reflexión subsiguiente
me convenció de que se trataba de un arma de doble filo
o, si se quiere, de una victoria pírrica. Para eludir las
redes y trampas de la censura, me había convertido yo
mismo en censor. (...) La idea de deslindar los campos,

---

[1] Emir Rodríguez Monegal, *El arte de narrar: diálogos* [conversations with
various authors], Prisma (Caracas: Monte Ávila, 1968) pp.165–98
(pp.178–79).

[2] José María Blanco White was a nineteenth-century Spanish exile to
England whose writings were bitterly critical of the Spanish Establishment.
Goytisolo has translated a selection of his English works into Spanish and
written in the prologue of the remarkable similarity between his own and
Blanco's experiences. *Obra inglesa de José María Blanco White*, 3rd edn
(Barcelona: Seix Barral, 1982).

> de dejar al censor su trabajo y cumplir yo el mío sin
> preocuparme con su existencia se abrió lentamente
> camino.[3]

There is a third feature of *Campos*, which along with its sibling *La Chanca*, reflects the watershed period of the author's career when they were written. From the committed nature of the early period, Goytisolo would move to a new attitude of privileging linguistic and literary revolution over straightforward documentary-style political protest. Again, in *Campos*, the changeover is discernible, with the subtle mixture of both modes of writing.

To make the transition while writing travel narratives was an apposite choice, as we shall see, for by its nature this genre is a hybrid creature that lends itself to a range of ambiguities, ambiguities exploited to the full by Goytisolo. For this reason, it is useful, before considering *Campos de Níjar* in isolation, briefly to survey the genre itself, in order to provide a background against which to place the text. How does Juan Goytisolo's account of a few days' journey in southern Spain fit into the corpus of travel writing, which stretches back for centuries and spans the globe? The rest of this chapter will attempt to answer this question.

Chapter 2 of this Guide will take up the subject of the author's attitude to Andalusia and its people, a recurrent and significant presence in his writing, both fictional and autobiographical. Some consideration will be given as to how this concern relates to his abiding affinity for social underdogs in general and, in particular, his subsequent interest in North African people and culture.

Chapter 3 will analyse the sophisticated interweaving of subjective and objective perspective in *Campos de Níjar*, looking also at how this issue intersects with the lyricism of certain passages of the text. Leading on from the question of perspective, Chapter 4 will examine aspects of the narrator's depiction: how he is made sympathetic, how and when he intervenes either noticeably or

---

[3] Juan Goytisolo, *En los reinos de Taifa*, 2nd edn (Barcelona: Seix Barral, 1986), pp.25–26. Further references will be given in the text, using the abbreviation *RT*.

unobtrusively, what the effects of this treatment are on the text as a whole.

Chapter 5 will take up the interplay between fact and fiction in the work: how they are combined, where the grey areas lie and what effect they have. Chapter 6 will analyse the subtle use of tenses in *Campos*, often unconventional and significant, together with the alternation between first- and third-person forms, and the handling of dialogue. Finally, Chapter 7 will compare the text with Goytisolo's other Andalusian travel book, *La Chanca*, in order to contrast the balance in each of documentary and literary components, and the extent to which these can co-exist without harming one another.

*

There is no clear-cut and universally accepted definition of travel narrative: it can be factual reportage, but also fiction and even romance; a subjective — but also objective — account of a journey; its focus may be trained on the traveller's experiences and reactions, but at the same time it may present the history and geography of the surroundings and their natives.

Perhaps one reason for the protean nature of the genre is its multiple overlap with other forms of literary expression. It has been seen, for example, as a 'sub-species of memoir in which the autobiographical narrative arises from the speaker's encounter with distant or unfamiliar data'.[4] On the other hand, an equally convincing case can be made for the genre as elder brother of the novel itself: both, one may observe, have traditionally sought to clothe the workings of the literary imagination in the trappings of veracity and trustworthiness, to give the reader adequate grounds for suspension of disbelief, to balance plausibility against excitement, entertainment against instruction. In terms of structure, too, travel writing has much in common with the conventional novel: the basic itinerary of the journey could be seen as analogous to the central story-

---

[4] Paul Fussell, *Abroad: British Literary Traveling Between the Wars* (New York: Oxford University Press, 1980), p.203.

line, with historical or other interpolations as well as detours and hold-ups having their parallel in the novel's customary twists and turns.[5] Indeed, confirmation of this is to be found in the great number of novels that actually use a journey as their central structuring principle, ranging from *Don Quixote* to contemporary works like Alison Lurie's *Foreign Affairs*. In both cases, the author utilizes a pattern of departure at the beginning, developments of various kinds in the course of the journey, and an ending that consists of an older and wiser homecoming, which is a conception identical to the structure of the traditional travel narrative.

Utopian fiction and its negative counterpart, dystopianism, are also close relatives of travel narrative.[6] Not only do they typically employ the premise of an account of a journey to a hitherto undiscovered land, they also utilize a device that is equally crucial to travel literature, namely, the contrasting of the traveller's home society — tending to resemble the reader's — with the one s/he is in the process of exploring, significantly different from narrator's and reader's. Thomas More's *Utopia*, which created the genre along with the word, is just such an account of a journey, by a European like ourselves, who is therefore in a position to highlight the most interesting divergences between us and the Utopians. As the title indicates, Jonathan Swift's *Gulliver's Travels*, a dystopian satire, is also structured as travel writing. A final example is to be found in Samuel Butler's *Erewhon*, at the beginning of which the narrator goes to considerable lengths to convince us that this is the non-fictional account of a journey, not the satirical utopian/dystopian construct that it soon reveals itself to be.

In all these relationships between the travel genre and other forms of literature — and one could cite others too: initiatory quest romance, picaresque, chivalric — there is cross-fertilization. It is

---

[5] Percy G. Adams, *Travel Literature and the Evolution of the Novel* (Lexington: University Press of Kentucky, 1983), especially p.206.
[6] The term dystopianism is used to describe works like George Orwell, *Nineteen Eighty-Four* (1949); that is to say, novels which take the ingredients of a traditional utopian construct and reveal them as night-marish, thus making an imaginary society horrific rather than desirable.

not only the utopian writers, for example, who have drawn on the conventions of travel literature, but also the travel writers who have exploited the devices of the utopian genre. One could cite Gerald Brenan's account of the years he spent in southern Spain after the First World War. Like a utopian writer, he takes a principle considered logical and universally right in our own society and shows how it may in fact be culture-bound, by demonstrating its inapplicability in the foreign society that he is describing. In *South from Granada*, this is the belief that it is important and good that people everywhere should be able to read and write. Brenan asserts:

> In our village there was nothing to read, so that even those who had learned soon forgot again because there were so few occasions for putting their knowledge into practice. [...] But what did this ignorance matter? The people of Yegen knew everything that was needed for their prosperity and happiness, and would have gained nothing but a few pedantic phrases from knowing more.[7]

This might be compared to Butler's device in *Erewhon*, where our universally agreed principles that crime is wrong, but illness is merely unfortunate, are reversed so that people are thrown into jail for being sick and sympathetically cured if they have an attack of stealing, say. Thus, the travel writer utilizes the utopian's method of warning the reader against mistaking culture-bound standards for universal ones.

As well as overlapping with these literary genres, travel narrative shares some ground with what are commonly considered to be non-literary forms of expression, notably socio-political writing and investigative journalism, in addition to perhaps the most obvious link of all: the guide-book. It has been noted that travel accounts are very often a discovery of the life of a lower social class by a more privileged narrator, just as much as an exploration

---

[7] Gerald Brenan, *South from Granada* (Cambridge: Cambridge University Press, 1988) p.65.

of an area unfamiliar by virtue of its physical distance from home.[8] Where this aspect is a significant component of the text's effect, the impact may be heightened by proximity rather than diminished by it. To discover shocking deprivation or injustice close to home, to discover that a completely alien way of life is the norm on our very doorstep may be more remarkable than being told that this is what happens on the other side of the world. Hence, where the class element does come into play — and especially when a text is critical of the treatment of certain members of society — the exoticism provided by geographical distance diminishes in importance, to be replaced by social distance.

Travel writing generally overlaps to some degree with the content of a guide-book about the same place, just as, conversely, a guide-book may well slip in a personal remark by its compiler or even a quotation from a literary work. Perhaps the only safe distinction to be drawn here is, as Paul Fussell observes, the readership for which each type of text is designed. 'A guide book is addressed to those who plan to follow the traveler. [...] A travel book [...] is addressed to those who do not plan to follow the traveler at all' (p.203).

*

Campos de Níjar takes few liberties with the literary genre, however outspoken it may be (albeit implicitly for the most part) in its socio-political commentary on the region it describes. On the contrary, Goytisolo makes maximum use of the traditional features of travel writing, rather as the skilled poet may write a beautiful and original sonnet without breaking any of the rules of scansion. He exploits the ambiguities of the genre's relationship with both fiction and fact, as well as with personal and impersonal forms of writing. And with the political implications of the different social classes he meets and their reaction to each other and to the narrator's status, he master-

---

[8] Joanne Shattock, 'Travel Writing Victorian and Modern: A Review of Recent Research', in *The Art of Travel: Essays on Travel Writing*, ed. Philip Dodd (London: Frank Cass, 1982), pp.151–64 (p.152).

16   *Campos de Níjar*

fully combines the exoticism of proximity through class difference
on the one hand, with the almost foreign, almost even non-
European status of Andalusia for the northern Spaniard.

The narrator of the text, like the author, is a native of northern
Spain now living in France, which places him in a position of
enormous superiority in the eyes of the downtrodden locals;
Catalonia's wealth compared with Andalusia's poverty, combined
with the political freedom and workers' rights known to exist
beyond the Pyrenees, bestow upon him an identity approaching the
very incarnation of all the dreams of self-betterment cherished by
the Nijareños. And yet he remains a Spaniard like them, despite the
yawning gulf of privilege. Is he therefore an outsider because of his
relative wealth, his different regional origin, and his émigré status?
Or does his native command of Spanish and his upbringing within
the borders of the same country make him a local guide? There is no
clear answer to this question, which will be discussed further in
Chapter 4; however, one may already observe that this ambiguous
position is not unique; it resembles, for example, that of
V.S. Naipaul writing about Trinidad, described by a critic as
'curiously hybrid, (…) since he comes as an outsider to write about
his own part of the world'.[9]

However, there is an additional poignancy in *Campos de
Níjar*, arising from the strength of regional, as opposed to national,
allegiances in Spain. To be a Catalan in Andalusia is perhaps to be
more of a foreigner than to be a Moroccan there, and to be an
Andalusian in Catalonia — the dream of so many still at home — is
surely to be more of an alien in the eyes of the locals than to be
French. Hence care must be taken, especially by a non-Spanish
reader of the text, not to underestimate the foreignness of the
narrator to the locals, however much for his part he may wish to —
and even feel he does — belong and however strong his emotional
ties to them may be.

Nevertheless, once again, the narrator's position is not without parallel elsewhere. One might mention George Orwell and *The*

[9] John Thieme, 'Authorial Voice in V.S. Naipaul's *The Middle Passage*', in
The Art of Travel, pp.139–50 (p.141).

Road to Wigan Pier, in which the English North-South divide could perhaps be considered comparable (though in reverse, of course) to the differences in wealth between regions in northern and southern Spain. Some comments on Orwell's work apply equally to Goytisolo's:

> Within the first few pages, [...] Orwell has clarified [...] his identity, a visitor from the South. But [...] he is also intent on distinguishing his stance from that of fellow southerners. [...] [He] refuses to pretend that he, a southern traveller, has access to what [a] young northern woman, from a different class from his own, believes, thinks, and feels. [...] The stance Orwell promotes [...] acknowledges [... that] the middle-class person [...] should not pretend more knowledge of or intimacy with [the working] class than a traveller can have of a place he visits but to which he does not belong.[10]

Likewise, Goytisolo's narrator informs the reader on the second page of *Campos*, firstly, that he is from Catalonia and secondly, that his attitude towards the southerners differs from the classic superior and derisory one: 'A través de sus hombres y mujeres que fueron a buscar trabajo y pan a Cataluña, [...] la quería [a Almería] sin conocerla aún' (10, 46). As far as the class barrier is concerned, Goytisolo, also like Orwell, refuses to indulge in the fallacy of empathy with the impoverished Nijareños, avoiding assumptions about how they think and feel, limiting himself to what they say and to the impression they make on the narrator.

*

If *Campos de Níjar* fits quite comfortably with twentieth-century travel writing in English, such as that of Naipaul and Orwell, can the same be said of its relationship with Spanish works within the

---

[10] Philip Dodd, 'The Views of Travellers: Travel Writing in the 1930s', in *The Art of Travel*, pp.127–38 (pp.132 and 134–35).

genre? Does it follow in the tradition of the writers of the Generation of 1898, whose travel books have been characterized as
'básicamente costumbrista', with the driving force behind them
being 'la búsqueda de la esencia del hombre de la meseta' (*2*,
p.415)? Or does Goytisolo opt to continue in the vein of Ramón J.
Sénder's generation, with an 'énfasis informativo, [...] a expensas
de la elaboración artística, de modo que se queda a la altura de la
crónica testimonial' (*2*, p.416)? Or, finally, does he follow the post-
war revival of the genre by Camilo José Cela and his *Viaje a la
Alcarria*, where 'en lugar de la realidad precisa, documental, [Cela]
ofrece una visión de la Alcarria que es el resultado de una transformación artística', where 'se trata del peculiar de Cela y no de sus
interlocutores', and where 'se trata de una pintoresca realidad
hispana, magníficos "tipos" que se convierten en figuras literarias'
(*2*, pp.419–20)?

The answer to all of these questions is yes and no, for *Campos
de Níjar* shares certain but never all elements with its various
Spanish forebears. Like the Noventayochistas, Goytisolo has
adopted a region and taken it to his heart; for them it was Castile,
for him it is Almería, but in either case, there is the important
common idea, expressed at the beginning of *Campos*, that 'la patria
chica puede ser elegida' (10, 46), that, in other words, one is not
forced by accident of birth to belong only to that unchosen place
where one happened to come into the world.

As for the documentary works of Sender's generation, it is
clear that Goytisolo's text is equally committed and that one of its
most powerful effects is to give a trustworthy-seeming and hard-
hitting picture of a region that is receiving unfair treatment from the
Madrid authorities, thus evincing the reader's indignation. Nevertheless, if it criticizes the contemporary Franco government for its
neglect of the region, it does not simplistically blame Níjar's plight
solely on a regime that has been in power for a couple of decades,
but rather 'it is clearly suggested as the product of actions and
attitudes dating back to the beginnings of modern Spain'(*6*, p.261).
If it seems inappropriate for a literary work to concern itself with
such matters, rather than leave it to the Sunday newspaper or a

television documentary, it is as well to recall that at the time of writing the mass media were too tightly controlled to function in this way, so that many creative writers of Goytisolo's generation felt honour-bound to fill the gap. Goytisolo has talked about 'la necesidad que sentíamos los autores de suplir el silencio de la prensa y de los medios de información española sobre situaciones reales del país'.[11]

Cela and Goytisolo are radically different writers as well as individuals, but it remains true that no less than *Viaje a la Alcarria*, *Campos de Níjar* is an affectionate and frequently lyrical depiction of the area, in which one often feels the narrator's sympathy towards the people and places he encounters: 'Tienen el rostro noble aquellos hombres. Una dignidad que transparenta bajo la barba de dos días y los vestidos miserables y desgarrados' (33, 63); 'Frutales y almendros alternan sobre el ocre de los jorfes y los olivares se despeñan por la varga lo mismo que rebaños desbocados' (43, 69).

It has been suggested that where *Campos* is perhaps most innovative with respect to other Spanish travel writing is in its primary focus on people rather than scenery: 'Esta idea supone una innovación considerable en la literatura española del género que, hasta la aparición de *Campos...*, había considerado la naturaleza como fin en sí que venía a constituir, además, el motivo central y casi exclusivo del libro de viajes. [...] En Goytisolo, [...] lo básico es el hombre, su modo de vida y costumbres'(*9*, p.117). However, this is just one point of view. It could also be argued that the text is constructed to create a fine balance of people against places, so that neither has pride of place, but each complements the other. Even if, as we have seen, the narrator informs us that his love for Almería sprang originally from his acquaintance with the people away from their landscape, the tone of the descriptions of scenery in *Campos* leaves us in little doubt that the narrator feels a fondness for it that is not wholly dependent on its inhabitants, but based on its autonomous esthetic charms too.

---

[11] Interview with José A. Hernández (1975), *Modern Language Notes*, 91 (1976), 337–55 (p.341).

*

Campos de Níjar is a far more challenging text than it may appear
on first reading. In the pages that follow, the reasons for this deceptive simplicity will be investigated, but in summary one may say
that very little is clear-cut and far more will be described as subtly
blurred, grey, interwoven. The plain described in Chapter 2 is
'difuminada por la calina' (17, 49); a better image for the effect of
the work as a whole could hardly be found.

2. Goytisolo and Andalusia

Andalusia and Andalusians have been an abiding presence in nearly all of Goytisolo's literature prior to *Reivindicación del conde don Julián* (1970), with only his first two novels *Juegos de manos* (1954) and *Duelo en el Paraíso* (1955) as significant exceptions. This chapter will examine what the motif represents in the corpus of the author's works, thus providing a background in which to place *Campos de Níjar*.

It is in his two-volume autobiography, *Coto vedado* (1985) and *En los reinos de Taifa* (1986), that we find a non-fictional, straightforward description of the affinity he feels towards the people of southern Spain and their region. The importance of this to him is highlighted by the key position —the ending of the first volume — and italic typeface accorded to the passage relating his first significant encounter with Andalusians, at the time of his military service, and with Andalusia, as soon as he was demobilized:

> *Una casualidad sumamente feliz y de consecuencias perdurables para ti determinó que la compañía a la que fuiste destinado de sargento estuviera compuesta en gran parte de murcianos y andaluces. [...] Su desamparo cultural y social, las burlas de que eran a veces objeto por parte de los demás te predisponían muy naturalmente en su favor. [...] El relato de su vida en [sus pueblos], de su belleza y atraso te conmovió.*[12]

The language in which the first trip to southern Spain is couched

---

[12] Juan Goytisolo, *Coto vedado*, (Barcelona: Seix Barral, 1985), pp.273–74. Further references will be given in the text, using the abbreviation *CV*.

could hardly be more exuberant; this is but a short extract:

> *Baño lustral, deslumbramiento epifánico : [...] afecto*
> *instintivo, espontáneo a un paisaje huérfano y suntuoso,*
> *nítida asunción del goce identificatorio, fulgurante*
> *anagnórisis de tu encuadre espacial : afinidad,*
> *inmediatez, concomitancia con una tierra casi africana*
> *que confiere al viaje el aura iniciática de una segunda,*
> *demorada natividad.* (*CV*, p.275)

However, in the second volume of the memoirs, Goytisolo describes his feelings towards some unskilled Valencian labourers with whom he mixed in Paris: 'En medio de mis compatriotas exiliados por razones económicas me sentía en España más que en la propia España, envuelto en una atmósfera de cordialidad, inmediatez y llaneza viva y estimulante' (*RT*, p.207). This could almost be a description of his feelings towards Almerienses and perhaps points to a more important source of empathy lying in Spanishness combined with working-class identity, rather than a stipulation that precise geographical origins must be Andalusian. Indeed, he recognizes this class element on the very same page: 'mi seducción intelectual y afectiva se desplegaba siempre ante hombres que no pertenecían a mi clase' and associates this with his homosexuality, which he had not yet consciously recognized: 'Dicha atracción innata, que otorga a la desigualdad social un papel muy similar, en el juego de lo complementario y opuesto, al que ejerce de ordinario la diferencia de sexo, se ahondaría y sexualizaría luego' (*RT*, p.207).

In the same work, he also explains the link that he feels between his affinity with southern Spain and his subsequent love for North Africa, alluding to 'ese calor, familiaridad y apoderamiento que de un modo instintivo, compensatorio buscaré y encontraré en el Maghreb' (*RT*, p.25). In an essay called 'La Chanca, veinte años después', he simply calls his relationship with North Africa the 'prolongación natural' (*4*, p.162) of his feelings for Níjar and La Chanca. What we may conclude, then, is that Goytisolo's affection for the people of Almería is emblematic rather than exclusive. There he finds working-class simplicity, unjust treatment worthy of sympathy, and southern warmth, but these features attract him when they occur elsewhere too, be it among a group of Valencian emigrés in Paris, or subsequently in his discovery of North Africa.

*

An important feature of Goytisolo's depiction of Andalusia is that it appears in juxtaposition with other regions and their inhabitants; indeed, the theme would lose much of its meaning if it were deprived of the contrast with Catalonia and the Catalans. He was born and raised in Barcelona, a city with a large non-native population from the South and his early social realist novels *Fiestas* (1958) and *La resaca* (1958) had dealt with the lives of this unfortunate underclass and the hostility towards its presence shown by the indigenous population, which was nevertheless enjoying a more comfortable existence partly owing to the cheap labour it was providing. If one considers *Campos de Níjar* in the light of this chronological development of the author's work, a bitter irony emerges, for once we have read the early novels, the Nijareños' desire to go to Barcelona is revealed as pathetically misplaced.

Around the time of writing the travel works, Goytisolo also produced some short fiction set in Andalusia and contained in the two collections *Para vivir aquí* (1960) and *Fin de fiesta* (1962). In the same vein was *La isla* (1961), written originally as a screenplay but ending as a long short story. Again, the Andalusians are rarely seen in isolation, but are juxtaposed with visitors to the region, be they bored, bourgeois Catalans or the eccentric Swedes who, incidentally, are also mentioned in *Campos* itself.

In 1966, *Señas de identidad* was published, the first, transitional step on the highly experimental path that Goytisolo would tread from then until the present. Here too, the plight of the southerners plays a part; we see them brutally taking out their frustration on a young bull at the local fiestas of Yeste and learn of the sad history of the surrounding area in the 1930s; we see fishermen

struggling to make a living in another southern village and hear
their stories of others who tried to go abroad but were the victims of
a confidence trick; and we encounter mainly anonymous Spanish
emigrés or economic migrants in France and, briefly, throughout
north-western Europe.

Taken all together, the attitudes of the southerners as
portrayed in the totality of Goytisolo's fiction are sadly circular: in
Campos and the other works that depict them on home ground, they
dream of going to Catalonia: 'Cataluña es el paraíso soñado por
todos los hombres y mujeres de Almería, una especie de legendario
y remoto Eldorado' (19, 50). In *La resaca*, where they are there,
they dream of emigrating to France. A character nicknamed Cien
Gramos asserts: 'En Francia podrás vivir como un señor, mientras
que aquí serás toa tu vía un don nadie' (p.856), while the lucky
Emilio who has gone to France confirms his old friends' vision by
writing in a letter: 'En Francia, el obrero no vive aislado, como
aquí. En Francia tiene el sindicato' (p.870).[13] When we actually see
the Spaniards abroad in *Señas*, however, they are full of nostalgia
for Spain, dreaming now of an idealized version of the home they
fled: 'tras evocar nostálgicamente el queso de Roncales, el lacón con
grelos y el chorizo de Cantimpalo, decretar, con unanimidad insólita
entre españoles, que agua pura y fresca y restauradora como la de
Guadarrama no había, pero que no señores, ninguna otra en el
mundo'.[14] Parenthetically one might note that these comments do
not happen to relate to southern Spain; nevertheless, the same type
of nostalgia is expressed by the Almeriense whom the narrator
meets at the beginning of *La Chanca*, so it would seem logical to
assume that this is meant to be representative of poor Spaniards in
foreign climes from whichever region of the country they may be.

---

[13] Juan Goytisolo, *La resaca* (1958), Aguilar *Obras completas*, 2 vols
(Madrid: Aguilar, 1977), I, pp.849–1030 (pp.856 and 870 respectively).
Note that this edition is not a complete works, but contains only Goytisolo's
writings prior to *Señas de identidad*.

[14] Juan Goytisolo, *Señas de identidad* (Barcelona: Seix Barral, 1980),
pp.251–52.

Thus, the comments of the locals in *Campos*, expressing their desire to move north to Barcelona, gain in significance and pathos if taken in the context of Goytisolo's depiction of the Andalusians and impoverished Spaniards in general throughout his fiction. What we see in this particular work is just one segment of a vicious circle suffered by a people doomed to misery: crushing poverty and deprivation if they stay in their native region, disillusionment and homesickness if they leave.

In the fiction written after *Señas*, the plight of the Andalusians, specifically, fades, but not the phenomenon that they exemplify: that of an ethnic group disadvantaged through no fault of its own, its members deemed inferior by more privileged western races, but its homeland and backwardness enjoyed exploitatively by the rich. In *Reivindicación del conde don Julián, Juan sin tierra* (1975), *Makbara* (1980), and *Paisajes después de la batalla* (1982), the same pattern is played out, with varying specificity as to the racial identity of the victims and the superior exploiters: Moroccans are the victims in *Don Julián*, with Spanish tourists the exploiters; in *Juan sin tierra*, Cuban slaves exploited by their Spanish colonial masters appear, together with an English tourist and Turkish pimp, to mention but two examples from that work. *Makbara* makes a North African of unspecified nationality and his lover, an androgynous creature, the underdogs, with Parisians and Americans playing the superior exploitative role. *Paisajes* draws generally on the immigrant population of Paris, with particular emphasis on the dark-skinned, as against the attitudes of the Parisian old guard towards them. *Las virtudes del pájaro solitario* (1988), shows the mystic as the victim of prejudice, which contrasts with the earlier ethnic emphasis, but nevertheless continues the concern for those perceived as diverging from a respectable norm of some kind and victimized for their otherness.

Whoever happens to play the part in a given work or episode, however, the underlying configuration remains the same and one that has been a recurrent preoccupation of Goytisolo throughout his writing career: this is the way in which the accident of birth imposes a position in the social hierarchy over which the individual has no

control. Whether it is the blind baby in *Campos*, physically handi-
capped because he happened to born into a family that could not
afford to have him cured, or the Cubans of *Juan sin tierra* born into
slavery, it is the same question of pure luck that fixes these people's
chances in life. Elsewhere than in *Campos*, the preoccupation is
viewed from the opposite position, namely, that of the person born
into a socially advantaged life, but wishing to identify with underdogs who nevertheless reject him for his social superiority (*8*,
pp.73–96). There is perhaps a glimpse of this in *Campos*, when the
narrator, despite his intense sympathy for the lot of the Nijareños, is
forced to admit that he can be no more than 'un espectador ajeno al
drama' (52, p.77), but although this thought causes him a sleepless
night, he is on balance surely pleased not to be doomed to the
misery of those he meets on his travels. In the mature fiction,
however, Goytisolo creates a protagonist-narrator, Álvaro Mendiola,
who goes so far as to call his privileged birthright his 'pecado de
origen', so much does he wish to join the ranks of the socially
and/or racially disadvantaged.

Thus the interest in and sympathy for the Andalusians in
Campos de Níjar is not a feature unique to that work, or even to that
period of the writer's career, but part of a continuum. As we have
seen, Goytisolo has always taken a literary, as well as personal,
interest in underdogs of all kinds, but to be an underdog is a relative
position; one must be under someone else, so it is logical that we
find these people appearing beside and in contrast to others more
fortunate, be it Andalusians beside the narrator of *Campos*, a
Catalan living in France, or Moroccans beside rich American sightseers in the later novels.

With respect to the disadvantaged position of the Nijareños
and their unirrigated desert-like region, as will later be the case with
the North Africans and their habitat, an uncomfortable contradiction lurks between the lines. On the one hand, *Campos de Níjar* —
and for the most part, the other works that depict the socially
disadvantaged too — are in that respect committed; they protest at
the injustice of the treatment of these people and express a clear
though implicit wish that the balance should be redressed. But on

the other hand, there is an equally unequivocal love expressed for the people and their country just as they are. Would the narrator of *Campos de Níjar* love going there so much if the locals lived in comfortable flats with washing-machines and cars, if the fields were as green as further north because proper irrigation had been brought to the region, if the Nijareños were all as sophisticated as himself because they had had access to the same standard of education, had the same opportunities to read and to travel? Surely not; Goytisolo is conscious of the same contradiction in himself as we sense in the character of his narrator, commenting in an essay:

> He vivido atrapado en un dilema insoluble: el que opone la visión estética y hedonista del mundo a un enfoque exclusivamente moral. Mi indignación ante las condiciones de pobreza y desamparo en que viven los hombres a quienes más cercano me siento [los andaluces] chocan de frente con la seducción íntima de un paisaje desnudo y áspero, de una serie de virtudes primitivas inexorablemente barridas por el progreso e industrialización. (*4*, p.163)

The problem, which is here recognized as without solution as far as the author's personality is concerned, was however to be resolved in his literature, by the simple expedient post-*Señas* of reserving the moral questions for subject-matter of non-fictional essays and articles, and allowing the fiction to concern itself primarily with esthetic, linguistic, and literary matters. In *Campos de Níjar*, though, the clash is still in evidence, as the protest element sits uneasily with the narrator's love of the primitive nature of the region and its people, this last coming uncomfortably close to the attitudes of rich northern European tourists choosing to holiday in a quaintly backward, unspoilt part of the world.

*

Campos de Níjar is about the scenery of a region as well as the
people that inhabit it, notwithstanding the opinion of certain critics
like Gonzalo Navajas: 'su interés primordial no es la descripción de
los lugares que el escritor recorre sino el hombre que habita en
ellos' (*9*, p.117). It would be pointless to speculate whether
Goytisolo finds the landscape beautiful because he is fond of the
people, or whether each is an independent judgement, but the fact
remains that a sizeable percentage of the work is taken up by what
one might call non-human description, more in quantity and finer in
quality, no doubt, than would be required simply to keep the censor
off the scent of the socio-political protest. In assessing his feelings
for Almería in an essay, moreover, Goytisolo gives as much weight
to the place as to the people, even mentioning it first: 'El atractivo
que su paisaje y su gente han ejercido sobre mí me ha marcado para
siempre'(*4*, p.162).

Here again, as with what draws Goytisolo to the people, it
would seem that the terrain's charms epitomize what he finds
attractive rather than standing alone and unique. It is hard to avoid
noticing how often a view is characterized as reminiscent of Africa
and/or desert-like; indeed, the rare glimpses of adequately watered
land receive dispassionate, informative description: 'Mi vecino me
enseña una huerta cercada con bardas. Dentro, alineados en
caballones y encañados cuidadosamente, hay bancales de judías,
tomates, berenjenas, pimientos' (15, 48). This stands in sharp
contrast to the pleasure clearly afforded to the narrator by contemplation of wilder country; a little further on, he revels in this more
muscular, vivid description: 'La llanura se extiende hasta los
médanos del golfo, difuminada por la calina. Los atajos rastrean el
pedregal y se pierden entre las zarzas y matorrales, chamuscados y
espinosos' (17, 49). In the later work *Makbara*, we find an evocation of North African scenery the tone of which confirms the
author's predilection for arid, wild desert: 'espacio ilimitado,
aislamiento, silencio, imbricación de olas y dunas, libertad

desmesurada y salvaje, nitidez, absoluta limpieza.'[15]

On turning to consider the features of urban description relished by the narrator, it is clear that the noise and bustle of a southern city are deemed preferable to sedate northern orderliness. On arrival in Murcia, he comments: 'Después del invierno gris del Norte, me sentía bien en medio de aquel bullicio' (11, 46). This is certainly an element of his character that he shares with the author, who has written repeatedly, and in different works, of the delights of chaotic city streets and squares, be they in the old quarter of Barcelona (*Señas de identidad*), Morocco (*Don Julián, Makbara*), Turkey (*Juan sin tierra*), or the neighbourhood of Paris where he lives (*Paisajes después de la batalla*). The colours and shapes of a southern town also play their part in the attraction Goytisolo feels; in an essay called 'Volver al sur', he refers to his 'fascinación íntima por unos pueblos adustos, recatados y blancos' (5, p.174). This is borne out in *Campos* by the care taken over details of description of the buildings in different towns and villages. In Rodalquilar, the narrator remarks that 'la iglesia, la escuela y la casa-cuartel de los civiles son edificios de construcción reciente, pobres y sin carácter' (24, 56). Níjar's houses are described in greater detail:

> Son de una sola planta y tienen las fachadas enjalbe-gadas pero, a diferencia de las de El Barranquete o Los Nietos, su aspecto es poco africano y recuerda más bien el de las viviendas de los pueblos de la Andalucía alta y Extremadura. El techo suele ser de teja encalada y, a través de las puertas siempre abiertas, se vislumbra el interior de los zaguanes. (43–44, 69)

San Miguel de Cabo de Gata again has its houses described: 'La imagen de Africa se impone otra vez al viajero. Las casas son rectangulares, blancas; semejan casi fortines' (71–72, 88). In San

---

[15] Juan Goytisolo, *Makbara*, 4th edn (Barcelona: Seix Barral, 1983), pp.205–06.

José, the narrator attributes the sad atmosphere partly to the condition of the houses: 'Es un pueblo triste, [...] con la mitad de las casas en alberca y la otra mitad con las paredes cuarteadas' (87, 100).

*

However much affection Goytisolo may feel for Almería and its people, feelings that he often projects onto the narrator of *Campos de Níjar*, a note of caution should be sounded before ending a chapter on the significance of southern Spain in his writings. He has chosen to identify with an area and a people of which he is not physiologically a native just as he has done latterly with the Maghreb; in this respect he demonstrates in his person an openness towards other cultures that he has often advocated in his writings. But he would not support blind local loyalty to Almería or anywhere else if it were at the expense of such openness: 'El cariño único, ensimismado y defensivo a lo "nuestro" — llámese español, francés, árabe, catalán, *euskera*, gallego o corso — y consiguiente desapego a lo ajeno no sólo empequeñecen el campo de visión y curiosidad humanas de un pueblo o comunidad, sino que falsean y anulan su propio conocimiento' (*3*, pp.135–36).

This attitude explains the narrator's disgust in *Campos de Níjar* — and similar characters appear with similar treatment in other works — at the type of person who shows precisely this type of stubborn, closed-minded loyalty for home. Whether it is national arrogance like that of the men at the beginning who drunkenly agree that 'España es el mejó país del mundo' (11, 47), or like that of the water-carrier at the end who self-deludingly asserts that in Spain 'se vive mejó que en ningún sitio' (124, 123); or whether it is regional, like Don Ambrosio's Castilian superiority complex — 'En Valladolid, [...] la gente es de otra manera' (109, 112) — the mentality is equally chauvinistic and xenophobic. Indeed, one of the reasons why the Nijareños appear by and large as sympathetic characters is surely that the majority of them do not praise their own heritage, but on the contrary are amazed that somebody fortunate enough to come from Barcelona and France should waste his time coming to visit them:

> — No habrá venío usté aquí por gusto, digo yo. [...]
> — ¡Anda! ¡Qué idea! [...] ¡Vení aquí desde Barcelona!
>   [...]
> — Largarse de Barcelona, tú... Con lo a gusto que
>   estaría yo allí. [...]
> — Si viviera en Cataluña es que no me asomaría yo por
>   Almería, vamos, ni que me mataran. (32–33, 63)

Thus there are several points to be taken into account when considering Goytisolo's attitude to southern Spain. One is that although it has a special place in his heart, when the characteristics that endear it to him appear elsewhere as has been the case with the Maghreb, he takes to such other places with similar enthusiasm. Second, one should be aware that class is at least as important as geographical origins, if not more so; the poor emigrés from Valencia are described in the memoirs with the warmth that one might have expected to find reserved for Almerienses, whereas we never find a portrayal of a member of the Andalusian upper class, suggesting that the author has no desire to meet and mix with such people, despite their regional identity.

Third, there is the contradictory factor of the author's moral position as opposed to his esthetic sensibilities; he is aware that it is wrong for the Almerienses to remain poor and backward, their country left running to desert, their beautiful coastline virtually undiscovered, yet it is this neglect which gives the place its majesty and the people their irresistible charm for him. When he writes in a recent essay both of the improvements in the standard of living there since he wrote his travel works and of what still remains to be done, the same contradiction emerges: 'El ausente, hoy, no halla los contrastes brutales que advertía antes: hambre, desnudez, analfabetismo, tracoma han desaparecido. Pero la conciencia apremiante del subdesarrollo le atenaza aún. Sentimientos de tristeza, *nostalgia* y, a veces, cólera frente a la terca iniquidad

española barajan con *una alegría vital matizada de remordimiento*'
(*4*, p.166; my italics). Yet it is perhaps this very tension between
indignation and affection that gives *Campos de Níjar* a dynamism
and vitality disproportionate to its measured pace and what is
superficially an uneventful narrative.

3. Subjectivity and Objectivity

This chapter will examine the exploitation of subjective and objective perspective in *Campos de Níjar*. Goytisolo manipulates these to great effect in the text, striking a fine balance that it is all too easy to miss. His subtlety in this regard perhaps explains the divergence amongst critics, whose opinions cover the whole spectrum of possibilities, ranging from claims of total objectivity to those who believe the work to be completely subjective. Santos Sanz takes the extreme view that 'el autor se ciñe al simple testimonio de la realidad. [...] La dimensión literaria de la obra es escasa y cuenta ante todo, como documento sociológico' (*12*, p.64). Gonzalo Navajas also seems to deny any subjective component, seeing the perspective as divided between pure objectivity on the one hand and the untainted subjective views of the Andalusians on the other:

> Por una parte [Goytisolo es] mediador objetivo e imparcial que registra el paisaje natural de Almería procurando omitir juicios o reacciones personales ante lo visto. [...] Por otra parte, es el transmisor que nos comunica los puntos de vista de los habitantes de Almería. (*9*, p.118)

He claims that Don Ambrosio's vision is the only exception to the 'perspectiva popular', as if Goytisolo's own northern, middle-class background, identical to that of his narrator, had nothing to do with the way *Campos* is presented.

For José Luis Cano, however, the work is 'una pintura [...] no exenta de ternura a veces, pero en general objetiva' (*1*), whilst Héctor R. Romero's appraisal juxtaposes objectivity with esthetics rather than the author's or the narrator's personal opinions and sentiments: 'A pesar del objetivismo de la narración, Goytisolo no puede rechazar su propio temperamento poético y, junto al lirismo de muchas descripciones, encontramos también una técnica marcadamente impresionista' (*11*, p.80). Like Romero, Kessel Schwartz sees objectivity as mitigated by the esthetic value of the text, saying that while Goytisolo includes 'some objective, almost photographic reproductions of the reality he is conveying', he also converts that reality 'into a novelistic and lyrical experience' (*14*, p.121). Gonzalo Sobejano sits in the middle ground, choosing his words carefully but perhaps somewhat presumptuously; Goytisolo's travel writings, he says, 'tratan de ser reportajes económico-sociales', and he adds that despite their 'realismo escueto', they are 'no exentos [...] de rasgos novelescos ni de tintes apasionados' (*15*, pp.360–61). He does not explain how he knows what they are trying to be.

Other critics see *Campos de Níjar* as more subjective than objective. Pablo Gil Casado says: 'Aunque se pretende que la visión es total e imparcial, por lo general no lo es, porque en relación con las condiciones de vida y el ambiente, el autor ve únicamente lo que le sirve para la crítica y el testimonio' (*2*, p.428). Genaro J. Pérez goes furthest in classifying the narrative stance of the text as subjective, saying that Goytisolo 'is highly subjective in what he shows' and going on to explain that his technique 'is to present a totally "involved-observer" in the travelogue, one dramatically opposed to the [traditional] travel narrator, who objectively provides a painting of the landscape and the people he encounters' (*10*, pp.97 and 101). Finally, Michael Ugarte's verdict is unequivocal: 'The word *objectivism* is, in the last analysis, a misnomer, for not only are Goytisolo's travelogues written from the point of view of one individual, a *yo*, but their existence in literature is the result of an ideological posture' (*16*, p.19).

What lesson can be drawn from this lack of a critical consensus? It would seem most reasonable to conclude that the position taken by Goytisolo as regards objectivity in *Campos de Níjar* is far more complex than it might at first seem. It is possible to agree at least in part with most of the differing critical appraisals, which suggests that there are many types of objectivity and subjectivity interwoven in the text. Those critics who take an extreme view may have drawn out just one thread which, although present, is not the only one that makes up the fabric of the discourse. This chapter will take a closer look at some of the most prominent of these threads, as well as the way in which they are woven together and the effects so produced.

First of all, let us consider Goytisolo's vocabulary. Does he limit himself to words devoid of emotional charge and which do not entail personal value judgements? As the very first sentence of the text shows, he certainly does not: 'Recuerdo muy bien la profunda impresión de violencia y pobreza que me produjo Almería' (9, 45). Here, one might argue, he is being openly subjective, announcing that this is a personal impression. Those in the objective camp might claim that he does not use language tainted by sentiment or judgement when he is describing the scenery and people of the region. However, such an argument is obviously untenable, as third-person descriptive passages are peppered with what could be termed weighted vocabulary. The houses of Rodalquilar, for example, 'son chatas, feas' (24, 56), not 'me parecen', though of course ugliness, like beauty, is in the eye of the beholder. Just beforehand, the reader has been told that 'el silencio es agobiante' (24, 56), not 'me agobia'. And the people whom the narrator meets on his travels are not exclusively described in neutral terms either: one woman 'aunque tiene el rostro seco y el vientre deformado por la maternidad es todavía bonita', for example (44, 70), a description that conveys both the narrator's warmth towards her and his compassion.

In short, Goytisolo's vocabulary in *Campos* expresses his narrator's feelings and opinions about the locations and people he depicts, even when he does not repeat explicitly that he is giving a personal view. However, Jesús Lázaro's accusation of 'falso objetivismo' (7, p.12) seems unfair; after all, the whole premise of the text is that a traveller is describing a journey that he made, conveying his impressions of the region and its inhabitants. At no point does it claim to be neutral or objective — indeed the first sentence, quoted

above, seems to do just the opposite — so why impose objectivity as
a criterion? Surely it is unnecessary, and moreover would be to the
artistic detriment of the text if every observation had to begin with
'me parece que' or some such reminder that the work is a personal
response to Níjar.

If it is not the author's choice of words that has given so many
critics the idea that *Campos* is on the whole an attempt at objectivity
(whether or not mitigating elements are observed), we must look for
other justifications of their claim. Perhaps it is based on the
component of the text that resembles a guide-book, the background
interpolated by the narrator or his interlocutors, which is neither
descriptive nor narrative but informative. Examples are the narrator's comments about local wines and drinking habits: 'A diferencia
del gaditano o malagueño, el almeriense es poco aficionado a la
bebida. La culpa se la echo yo a los caldos del país, por lo general
muy medianejos' (25, 59). At this point, there is even a footnote
excepting Albuñol wine from the generalization, a device that
heightens the atmosphere of impersonal, factual commentary. A
similar register is to be found at intervals in the text, when, for
example, the narrator explains the need for trees in Almería (19,
53), or talks about the ceramics of Níjar (48, 72). Sometimes he
adopts the guide-book tone to provide historical background, as
when he arrives at San José: 'Arruinado por la crisis minera de
principios de siglo, no se ha recuperado todavía del golpe y vive,
como tantos pueblos de España, encerrado en la evocación huera y
enfermiza de su esplendor pretérito' (87, 100–01). Of course, none
of this type of commentary is devoid of personal opinion, but that
need not detract from its status as explanatory background, which
imbues the text with a certain documentary flavour; it is one thread
in the fabric of the text that seems to have caught the eye of the
objective camp of critics.

Another may be the inclusion of photographs and a map. The
latter, like the guide-book comments, serves an informative purpose,
providing the reader with a factual basis of knowledge about the
region and also establishing the narrator's status as truthful and
well informed on his subject: a reliable guide. The photographs, on

the other hand, are a debatable element: they may corroborate the descriptions, but may do just the reverse if, for example, the reader finds that the houses in the picture of Rodalquilar are not ugly. Photographs seem to add objectivity to the work, but it is worth remembering that there is a photographer who is choosing where to point the camera and an editor who is deciding which pictures to select for inclusion. Hence, photographs selected by an individual are arguably just as subjective as the words one may choose to describe their content.

Reported speech in abundance, as we find in *Campos de Nijar*, can also create an impression of objectivity. The narrator seems to become the silent transcriber who simply passes on what he has heard without embellishment. As with the photographs, though, this idea of straight reproduction is shown on further reflection to be false. In the first place, there is once again the influence exerted by selectivity: which comments are worth transcribing and which are not? And in the second place, direct speech is ultimately Goytisolo's creation, no matter how faithfully it may reflect or mimic conversations that could have taken place in real life. Furthermore, it is the author who has decided how much dialect to put into the locals' mouths: enough to convey something of the sounds and rhythms of local speech, but not so much as to risk unintelligibility or ungainliness. He has chosen where to employ direct and where indirect speech, which is to say, how much the reader should hear voices and how much learn just the content of what people think. Chapter 5 of this Guide will examine the status of *Campos* as fiction or non-fiction and Chapter 6 will analyse the dialogue in more detail, but for the time being, suffice it to say that dialogue comes from Goytisolo's pen just as descriptive passages do; even taken as an honest attempt by the author to provide opinions other than his own - which is highly debatable — they have been selected by him as representative and relevant and they have been subjected to artistic elaboration, conscious and unconscious.

Therefore, objectivity emerges as a literary technique, an effect created by a skilful writer at given moments in the text —

when he gives what has been called guide-book background, when
he puts in photographs and a map, when he uses direct speech - and
not an intrinsic, natural characteristic of *Campos de Níjar* as a
whole. It is worth reiterating, however, that there is no reason for
seeing this either as a trick played on the naïve reader by the
cunning writer, or as a shortcoming of the work, because nowhere
does Goytisolo claim to be objective; on the contrary, he keeps
reminding us of the traveller-narrator's presence as an individual.
Furthermore, there is no universal law of literature, or even of travel
literature, which states that the more objective it is, the better. In
fact, it would seem more reasonable to agree with Percy Adams,
who argues that a key element of travel writing is precisely the
interweaving of the personal perspective with external reality:

> Throughout history, [... travel] literature has been a
> combination of the objective and the subjective, of
> details of setting, history, and customs to go with the
> traveler's own experiences, adventures, and reflections.
> [...] This tension between the personal and the imper-
> sonal [...] is as important in the evolution of travel
> literature as it is in the evolution of the novel.[16]

As we saw at the beginning of this chapter, several critics juxtapose
objectivity with the lyricism of *Campos de Níjar*. The implication
seemed to be that if the work was lyrical, then objectivity would
have to be sacrificed to some extent. It is hard to see why this should
necessarily be true: many accomplished novels written in Spain in
the 1950s, the decade in which objective social realism was in
vogue, appear to prove the contrary. Rafael Sánchez Ferlosio's *El
Jarama* (1956) is accepted as a fine work of literature with many
beautiful lyrical passages as well as a shining example of how
effective a device objectivity can be. Goytisolo himself wrote several
worthwhile novels in this style, including *Duelo en el Paraíso*

---

16 *Travel Literature*, pp.108–09. This runs counter to Genaro Pérez's assertion, quoted
above, that traditional travel writing is objective.

(1955), where lyrical passages in no way undermine the objective style. However, in the specific context of *Campos de Níjar*, the observation is an interesting one, suggesting that the most lyrical elements of the text are those that do not attempt to be or to seem objective. Let us therefore consider whether lyricism in the text is connected significantly with the question of objectivity and if so, whether they are mutually exclusive or undermine one another in any way.

The threads of apparently objective discourse woven into the fabric of *Campos* have proved to be chiefly those that provide informative background concerning local customs and history. Are these lyrical in any sense? The examples commenting on the wines of Almería and the mining crisis, cited above, are not lyrical in style and would therefore seem to support the contention that lyricism and objectivity do not coincide in the text. But on looking further afield, counter-examples can easily be found:

> La sierra es ocre, desértica. Su vegetación se reduce al palmito, que los almerienses emplean para fabricar escobas y esteras, y cuyo cogollo, blanco y sabroso, se consume, importado de Africa, en todos los países de Europa, donde es más estimado que el espárrago.
>
> Media hora de camino por curvas cerradas y el faro de la Testa del Cabo aparece de pronto, uno de los más hermosos faros del mundo, sin duda. Las montañas lo aíslan enteramente de tierra y, batido día y noche por el mar, se yergue, solitario y agreste, atalayando la costa del moro, vigía fiel, hoy, de tempestades y naufragios, ayer, de desembarcos berberiscos. (77, 94)

The guide-book components of this extract are, first, that the Almerienses use the dwarf-palms to make brooms and mats, and second, the lighthouse's history and present function. And yet the passage is a fine example of lyrical description too: the words 'escobas y esteras' lilt alliteratively, and the identical syllable numbers and stress patterns of 'tempestades y naufragios' on the one hand and 'desembarcos berberiscos' on the other create a rhythmic balance in the present and past fortunes of the lighthouse.

Not only can the most apparently objective strands of the text be lyrical, then, but also, contrary to what is suggested by the critics who see lyricism as incompatible with objectivity, the most overtly personal aspects of *Campos* are often the most prosaic. It is precisely when the narrator is telling us which buses he caught or missed, what time he awoke and other such indisputably individual, anecdotal facts, that the discourse is furthest from lyricism. The narrative content of the text will be discussed presently, but for the time being, consider the ending of Chapter 3: 'Yo estoy algo cansado de la caminata y les paso el paquete de Ideales. Las casas de Níjar apuntan detrás de la loma. El cielo bulle de pájaros y reanudamos la marcha' (40, 68). Arguably, the only lyrical moment here is the use of 'bullir' for birds, which occurs just when the personal element of the passage is momentarily suspended; the rest is couched in simple, everyday Spanish. And one could cite similar examples throughout the text. In other words, if objectivity and lyricism are connected at all in *Campos*, the relationship is harmonious; it is subjectivity that seems most hostile to poetic language.

The matter becomes more complex, however, on investigation of the descriptions where the reader's attention is not particularly drawn to the personal focus, but where, as was observed above, the vocabulary is weighted emotionally or judgementally. For the most part, these passages are not lyrical but, rather, evocative; with simple syntax and skilful verbal economy, a few well-chosen details will conjure up a whole atmosphere or scene: the heat, some names of plants, an old lorry bumping along, for example, will convey mood at least as effectively as poetic flights of fancy. The exception to this deliberately and strikingly sparse style is Goytisolo's use of imagery in the text. Although simply worded, this imbues the descriptions with an air of poetic sensitivity and creativity while avoiding any risk of embellished language, which might seem pretentious.

Gonzalo Navajas finds Goytisolo's use of imagery sparse, 'de manera que la imagen no asfixie nunca al tema y lo relegue a segundo término, sino que sirva estrictamente para reforzarlo' (*9*, p.120). However, it is far more widespread than his use of lyricism. Perhaps it is unobtrusive precisely because of the simple language in which it is expressed and because images are rarely developed or extended: 'Las montañas se interponen entre el llano y el mar como gigantescas bestias acostadas y amurallan el horizonte con su testuz alto, sus grupas redondas, sus lomos macizos y lisos' (86, 100). This is the most extended image that Goytisolo uses and is perhaps less effective than the inspirational flashes which inject vivacity and sometimes even drama into descriptions of scenery that might otherwise become repetitive, especially given that the narrator makes slow progress through landscapes that he keeps telling us are desert-like, and through villages that keep reminding him of each other for their African appearance and abject poverty.

The most exciting images are like lightning flashes that jolt the account out of any danger of giving featureless scenery an equally featureless description. By way of contrast with the rather ponderous example quoted above, consider how lively the following unexpected image is in its brevity: 'El mar está rizado como un campo de escarola' (94, 104). Although there are a few cases of quite commonplace imagery — a pile of salt looking like snow (76, 93), a thick curtain of trees (111, 114) — Goytisolo's images are more often imaginative and unusual, sometimes almost surreal, as when a line of telegraph poles is likened to the teeth of a comb (111, 114), or beached boats to dead insects (72, 88).

Near the beginning of Chapter 2, Goytisolo describes the sea when calm as 'una franja de plomo derretido' (17, 49). Again, the rapidity with which he moves on is striking; the next sentence has nothing to do with the sea any more but instead presents another fleeting image: 'A la izquierda, las cordilleras parecen de cartón.' And the sentence after that is on another subject again, unconnected with either of the preceding two. The effect of these flashes of imagery is that of transient impressions and ideas. The narrator's train of thought is conveyed to us as we follow his gaze passing swiftly from sea to mountains and on. However, as well as communicating the traveller's movement as he goes on his way looking this way and that, these flashes of metaphor and simile provide an insight into the author's fertile imagination. No matter how much he may seem to be modestly keeping himself out of the limelight, focussing on the people and places around him and not on himself, his images point in two directions at once: they do evoke the scenery and atmosphere powerfully, but they also reveal the creativity of their inventor. The narrator's persona will be the subject of Chapter 4 of this Guide but let us note that, by its very nature, imagery is a subjective phenomenon, reflecting an individual's creative mind. As soon as something is reminiscent of something else, it points to the mental associations and idiosyncrasies of a particular person. A windmill, for example, resembling 'una flor de pétalos inmensos y abarquillados' (112, 114) or, for that matter, seen as a giant, reflects the mentality of the beholder, be they Goytisolo's imaginative traveller or the deranged Don Quixote. If imagery is a feature of lyricism, which we found to be compatible with apparently objective discourse in *Campos*, it must nevertheless be acknowledged that it does subtly betray the presence of an individual mind behind the text.

Several threads of subjective and objective elements in *Campos* have now emerged. On the objective side, there has been the guide-book component of the work: a map, historical background, details of local wines, customs, crafts. One could also have mentioned the descriptions of food, dress, and music. But these are often presented prominently by the traveller: his own itinerary is marked on the map, he is the one drinking the wine and tasting the food, so even these are given a personal angle. Also tending to objectivity have been parts of the descriptions of what he sees around him, but again, these have been shown to be peppered with vocabulary expressing personal opinions and feelings: the houses of Rodalquilar were ugly; at Testa del Cabo was 'uno de los más hermosos faros del mundo'. And an appearance of objectivity provided by the abundance of direct speech was noted, but it had to be admitted that this must at the very least have been tailored by the author, slanted through selectivity, and that in the final analysis, it was his creation just as much as anything else within the covers of the book. Similarly, the photographs appeared to be objective corroboration of the written descriptions, but they too had been chosen for inclusion and were therefore unlikely to contradict the picture of the region that the author sought to convey.

Unexpectedly, it emerged that the lyrical passages in the text need not clash with the limited objectivity that it contained, but the imagery in particular, often inspired and arresting, was bound to tie description implicitly to the individual mind that created the text.

Having examined Goytisolo's descriptive techniques and considered the status of dialogue in the light of the objectivity/ subjectivity question, we have one last component of *Campos* to explore, namely, the narrative. It may not be a full-blown plot in the conventional sense, with suspense and development of intrigue, but the text does tell the story of the traveller's journey, complete with anecdotal details like his not being able to fall asleep one night (52, 77) and his oversleeping the following morning (55, 78). And there is a neat structure of arrival in Almería at the beginning and departure at the end, with the traveller's daily itinerary providing a backbone for the intervening chapters.

One might think that this element of the work would be the most indisputably subjective one. And yet, curiously enough, this is perhaps where an objective technique is most effective. It is when the narrator is describing the specific vicissitudes of his travels that he appears most convincingly as the neutral chronicler, able, as far as is humanly possible, to exclude personal opinion from his account. Here are some examples of narrative sentences; it is worth noting how much freer they are of weighted vocabulary than the descriptive ones that have been examined above:

> Cuando llegué a la central de autobuses, el coche acababa de irse. Como faltaban dos horas para el próximo, dejé el equipaje en consigna y salí a cantonear.
>
> (11, 46)

> Uno [meaning himself ...] se abandona al asperillo
> del vino y al regosto de la comida con un olvido tan
> completo de los que en el mundo ocurre que luego le
> hace avergonzarse. (52, 77)

> El de Fernán Pérez me había dejado en el cruce de
> Níjar y San José y, durante una hora, permanecí al borde
> de la cuneta aguardándolo [the coach]. (121, 121)

It is true that the narrative of *Campos de Níjar* occupies far less
space than either the descriptive passages or the dialogue, but it is
nevertheless the structuring principle of the whole text, which gives
it an importance disproportionate to its volume and an influence on
the overall mood of the work more powerful than one might at first
realize. It would therefore seem to go some way towards providing
an explanation for the otherwise puzzling critical opinion that
Campos is basically an objective work. Surely it is the calmly
neutral and dispassionate way in which the traveller recounts the
anecdotal details of his trip — which buses he took, which
cigarettes he smoked — that imbues the work with an objective
tone. As we have seen, however, this is deceptive, for when he
comes to depict the region and its people rather than his own
movements, subjectivity is strongly predominant; we should not be
taken in by a bus timetable or a sleepless night and jump to the
conclusion that if they are described objectively, the whole text must
be too. The objectively told narrative may be the backbone of
Campos de Níjar, but the flesh and blood — the landscape, the
people — throb with the vitality of a moving, personal vision.

4. The Narrator

'Any travel book requires generically that the narrator depict himself as likable' (*Abroad*, p.185). Whether or not this statement by Paul Fussell can be adequately supported in the general terms in which it is phrased need not concern us here, for there can be little doubt that in the case of *Campos de Níjar*, the narrator does indeed make himself likable. How does he achieve this? The answer would seem to lie in a number of elements of his character as this is portrayed in the text.

First, there is his undisguised sympathy for social underdogs:

> La cama es buena para quien tiene el estómago lleno y
> sabe que al día siguiente no habrá de faltarle lo
> necesario, pudiendo ir de un sitio a otro sin ser esclavo
> de ninguno, y mirar las cosas desde fuera, como un
> espectador ajeno al drama. Uno sabe [...] eso y, cuando
> apaga la luz, piensa en los otros. Las horas se suceden
> en el cuadrante del reloj y el sueño se le escapa. (52, 77)

Correspondingly, his odium for what he portrays as the exploitative and patronizing, non-native upper class of the region confirms our respect for his strong sense of natural justice. The representative of this group is Don Ambrosio, towards whom no antipathy is explicitly stated. However, the encounter takes place far enough on in the text for the reader to be convinced that if the narrator reports comments like the following, he cannot feel anything but disgust for the man:

> No son como nosotros, créame. En Valladolid, por lo
> menos, la gente es de otra manera. [...] En esta tierra,

> [...] muchas alharacas, sonrisas y, cuando uno se va, lo
> ponen como a un trapo. Son verdaderamente esclavos,
> se lo aseguro. Ganan cuatro cuartos y ya los tiene usted
> en la taberna, cantando y batiendo palmas. [...] Todo se
> les va en apariencia y fachada. (109, 112)

Add to this the sensitivity of his physical descriptions of scenery and
we have a very positive, unavoidably sympathetic character. Further
touches to the picture are the admission of endearingly human
failings: drinking too much, not liking to rise early, being unable to
contain tears or rage: 'La tempestad había desfogado su cólera y yo
seguía a cuestas con la mía. [...] Bebí un vaso [de Jumilla] y otro y
otro y el dueño de la taberna me miraba y, al acercarse a servirme
otra botella, me enjugué la cara' (125, 123–24).

One aspect of the narrator's character which enhances his
image is common to numerous protagonists of classic travel works:
this is his contempt for tourists and his care in drawing a sharp
distinction between himself and these lesser mortals (*13*, p.163).
Fussell notes that 'cruel mockery of tourists — often American — is
an important conventional element of the British travel book'
(*Abroad*, p.186). Whilst this may be true of British works,
Goytisolo's main victims in *Campos de Níjar* are French, though it
is worth noting parenthetically that he will attack American tourists
in his later novels *Reivindicación del conde don Julián* and
Makbara, and English and Spanish ones in *Juan sin tierra*. The
precise nationality seems less important than the underlying
implication that tourists are insensitive and destructive, and take an
exploitative attitude to their host resort, whereas travellers like the
narrator are just the opposite.

Let us look at the passage concerning the French tourists in
Campos. Mockery — though of a comparatively gentle nature — is
the abiding tone from the start and a tacit comparison with the
narrator is suggested repeatedly. These people are from Paris like
him, but they are travelling in their French car, protected from
direct contact with the Nijareños, rather than immersing themselves
in the local way of life by taking buses and hitch-hiking. We know

nothing about the narrator's attire, but judging by the way in which he pokes fun at the Frenchman's outfit, we can safely assume that he is dressed in a far less noticeable style: 'Va vestido como un explorador de película, con pantalones cortos de color caqui y camisa blanca. Sólo le falta el casco' (57, 80). The implication is that unlike him, they are treating the journey like a safari into uncharted jungle. Following immediately on this description of the clothes and the car, comes the man's comical question to the narrator — in pidgin Spanish mixed with French — of where water may be found. The narrator, on the other hand, replies in faultless French, reminding us that he, unlike them, is quite bilingual, a superior breed of traveller. He does not laugh at himself by transcribing a Spanish accent in French, yet he is likely to have one and moreover, is willing and able to write phonetic dialogue, as we have amply seen in the case of the local Spanish dialect.

Next comes the first appearance of the Frenchwoman. Her peeling nose indicates that she has been indulging in a touristic pursuit as trivial as sunbathing, or else that she cannot take the sun with her sensitive northern complexion. Either way, this places her in a position of inferiority relative to the narrator, who repeatedly mentions the strength of the sun, but is never harmed or deflected from his purpose by it. He can cope with the southern heat; she cannot. The Frenchwoman's anger and impatience make her almost a caricature of the nagging, comfort-loving wife, unable to appreciate the simple pleasures of 'les pays pauvres' (58, 80). The ending of the encounter, which consists of a three-way conversation between a local and the Frenchman, with the narrator interpreting, further emphasizes the contrast between him and the tourists; he, like a chameleon, able to communicate with both in their own idiom; they, deliberately enclosed in their French shell of a car and a language.

This episode is, then, carefully orchestrated to bring out the fact that the narrator bears no resemblance whatever to a tourist, depicted as a breed that ranges from the ridiculous though well-meaning — the Frenchman in his inappropriate clothes and inadequate Spanish — to the narrow-minded, superficial, and condescending, in the case of the woman.

With this attitude of the narrator towards tourism in mind, one may note another nail in the coffin of Don Ambrosio, for he is in favour of encouraging it. Worse still, this appears to be motivated purely by thoughts of his own profit, not even to improve the lot of his impoverished tenants: 'El día en que hagan la dichosa carretera, las casas cuadruplicarán de valor. En verano podré alquilarlas a los turistas' (98, 107).

Americans are not exempt from criticism in *Campos* either. They appear as a species closely related to the tourist and at least as despicable: the sailor on shore leave. Here again, the contrast with the narrator is implicit but no less striking for that. In Chapter VI, we learn that three drunken Americans had refused to pay their taxi-driver the previous evening, in revenge for which he had stripped them of their clothes and valuables (75, 92–93). Their loutish behaviour causes one of the locals to recall an earlier incident, when 'molieron a palos a un limpia' (75, 93). Now the context in which all this is revealed is a friendly meal in a *fonda*, at which the narrator has struck up a conversation with three local men. Here he is, breaking bread with them, enjoying their company and way of life on their own terms: 'Y sentados los cuatro hablamos de las cosas que pasan por el mundo y nos excitamos de tal modo que elevamos la voz, damos gritos y el patrón tiene que cerrar la puerta' (76, 93). And at the same time, here are we, learning how other visitors to the area are violent, dishonest, and boorish; in short, as one of the group says: 'Vienen aquí creyendo que tienen derecho a todo' (75, 93).

However, as we have seen, Goytisolo has admitted to a certain ambivalence on the subject of making the region more wealthy, which the arrival of tourism would accomplish, and these same divided feelings do briefly come across in *Campos* itself, when the narrator contemplates the beauty of the lighthouse of Testa del Cabo:

> Uno piensa con tristeza que un sitio así debería ser baza
> turística importante y contempla melancólicamente la

carretera estrecha, polvorienta y sinuosa, por la que
apenas cabe un automóvil, y cuyo acceso, para colmo de
la ironía está prohibido a los coches particulares que
—según leo en un cartel — no dispongan previamente
de permiso. (77–78, 94)

Is the sadness due to the fact that tourism could bring prosperity to
the region, but the infrastructure is lacking? This would represent a
perhaps surprisingly favourable attitude towards the industry, which
would almost resemble Don Ambrosio's, were it not for the fact that
the narrator has nothing to gain personally from this wish. Or is the
sadness rooted in his awareness that, sooner or later, the spot will be
discovered by the masses and will lose something of its charm in the
process? In literal terms, the text indicates that the first hypothesis
is correct, but between the lines there is perhaps a hint of the second
and the pain of the dilemma expressed in the essay.

Lastly, one must note that immediately following on these
observations about the lighthouse, the narrator provides a non-
critical view of one family of tourists. These are a Swedish couple
and child, never — significantly? — called 'turistas', but who are
camping in the area and speak no Spanish or any other language
permitting communication. Although they are isolated from the
local community because of this, the implication is at least that they
appreciate the beauty of the surroundings and do neither it nor
anyone any harm. They are depicted as eccentrics, but sympathetic
ones: 'los suecos deben ser algo locos', thinks the narrator, and the
local innkeeper concurs: 'Locos, sí; y mucho más de lo que usté se
figura' (78, 95).

It cannot be stated baldly, then, that the narrator is an enemy
of tourism *per se*; his attitude is nuanced to some degree, in much
the same way as the author's is. Nevertheless, the classic distancing
of himself from identification with tourism, to be found in
innumerable travel narratives, is also utilized in *Campos*, with the
effect of increasing our sympathy and respect for the narrator
through contrast.

The final important element of the narrator's character,

which, if not a reason to warm to him, is at least one to win our respect and trust, is his knowledgeability. He has made it clear in Chapter 1 that he is familiar with the area generally, from the frequent visits he has made there: 'salvando centenares de kilómetros, le rindo visita todos los años' (10, 46). He has made it his business to study the local history, geography, and traditions and frequently imparts informative snippets of one kind or another:

> Ocupada sucesivamente por fenicios, cartagineses, romanos, visigodos, Almería conoció un breve período de esplendor durante los albores de la dominación musulmana. [...] Desde su conquista por los Reyes Católicos la región ha sufrido una ininterrumpida y patética decadencia. (109, 112)

> La falta de árboles provoca una intensa erosión del suelo y explica que el nivel de precipitaciones de la región sea de los más bajos de España. Al suelo pedregoso y la sequía debe añadirse, aún, la acción sostenida del viento. (39, 68)

> Los hombres cantan. Sus tonadas, no obstante, recuerdan muy poco a las que se oyen en otras regiones de Andalucía. La letrilla es melancólica, una especie de lamento minero próximo a la taranta. (35, 65)

He has asked intelligent questions and learnt from what local people have told him. At the beginning of Chapter 2, for example, he listens, while travelling on a bus, to his neighbour's explanation of an experimental system of irrigation. But through his modesty he avoids appearing a know-all and thus alienating the reader. On the mining crisis of Almería, he comments:

> De las numerosas explicaciones que he oído acerca de su origen y causas posibles — incuria de los gobiernos, inadaptación a los modernos métodos de explotación, competencia industrial catalana, etc. —, ninguna me ha

satisfecho totalmente y, *esperando que alguien más indicado que yo las complete algún día*, invito a recorrer a los estudiosos los antiguos centros mineros de la provincia. (85, 99; my italics)

Hence we have a narrator with moral fibre and a strong sense of natural justice, but one who is also warm-hearted and emotionally sensitive both to the human misery he encounters and the esthetic beauty of its setting. He is to be respected for his intelligence and knowledgeability, but wins our affection for his character flaws and his modesty. He is an exemplary traveller — by contrast with the French tourists and American sailors — for his willingness and ability to integrate with the local way of life, even if both he and the reader are aware that this can only be partial due to the gulf of privilege that separates him from the Nijareños.

This last element of the narrator's integration depends heavily on the perspective of the text, however. It is because the narrative is presented through his eyes that we feel he has succeeded in coming close to the local population. One could imagine that the same story told by one of the lorry-drivers or barmen would depict him as far more noticeably an outsider, however likable and sympathetic. The narrator does recognize that he can only be an 'espectador ajeno', but precisely how 'ajeno' might well seem different according to which side of the divide one happened to be standing.

*

Perhaps the hardest question to address as far as the narrator is concerned is more fundamental than this, though. Simply put: is he Juan Goytisolo and if not, then who is he? Some consolation is to be had from finding the same problem arising in other travel narratives: speaking of Smollett's *Travels through France and Italy*, published in 1766, for example, a critic has observed that the narrator is:

'a persona, a figure who simultaneously is and is not
Tobias Smollett, a shaped projection of the author
moulded within certain literary conventions and to
certain literary ends. [...] Smollett and the Traveller
[...] may not be one, but they are Siamese twins, for the
most part making the same journeys, seeing the same
sights, meeting the same people.[17]

Who is not puzzled by the enigmatic identity of the narrator? He is a
man whose personal circumstances appear to tally with Goytisolo's,
but who is never named, and about whom one has learnt almost
nothing by the end of the text, except that he smokes and drinks,
finds it difficult to rise early, and is deeply moved by what he has
seen and heard in the course of his travels. And yet, paradoxically
perhaps, it is easy to gain the impression that he has been totally
frank with us and that when we close *Campos*, we now know him
intimately.

The phenomenon may be attributable to the narrator's use of
different tones at different points in the work, which vary the
distance he keeps between himself and the reader; we shall take
each in turn for the sake of clarity, but it is worth pointing out that
they do melt into one another to some degree.

The beginning of a text is of especial impact, for the reader is
likely to form a first impression and only reluctantly to modify it if
forced to do so. Goytisolo makes use of this human obstinacy and
opens *Campos de Nijar* with a seemingly non-fictional, open-
hearted, almost conversational account of the first-person narrator's
despairing love for the province of Almería and reasons for these
feelings. He refers, still in the first chapter, to his schooldays and
the tedium of learning the geographical names of the area by heart,
to his Catalan background where he first encountered Almerienses,
to impressions formed on previous visits to the region; all of this

---

[17] Peter Miles, 'A Semi-Mental Journey: Structure and Illusion in
Smollett's *Travels*', in *The Art of Travel*, pp.43–60 (pp.43–44).

gives the reader a sense of shared autobiographical intimacy with him. At the end of the chapter, he reverts to the present journey, reproducing two snatches of dialogue, one between locals and the other one in which, unusually, the narrator's speech is reported directly. Indeed, it consists of three sentences rather than the monosyllabic comments to which direct self-quotation — on the rare occasions when it is to be found at all — is generally limited elsewhere.

In other words, this chapter differs from the main body of the text in its portrayal of the narrator, first by providing personal details about his life beyond the few days of travel that are the subject of the book; second, by permitting the reader to hear his voice, rather than merely learn indirectly the import of what he has said.

Moving on from this maximum intimacy of the opening chapter, let us consider how the narrator depicts himself — or avoids doing so — as *Campos de Níjar* progresses. The beginning of Chapter 2 sets the tone for the majority of the work in this respect. The narrator starts by reporting a conversation with a man sitting next to him on the bus, but now the pattern is different: the words of the local are reported directly whereas the narrator's are given only in indirect form:

> Mi vecino [...] me pregunta si soy extranjero. Le respondo que soy de Barcelona y pronuncia unas palabras en catalán.
> —He trabajao allí casi diez años -dice. [...]
> —Fíjese usté.
> Mi vecino enseña una huerta. [...]
> —Son magníficos, ¿no?
> Digo que sí, que son magníficos. (15–16, 48)

It is worth noting the subtlety with which this device is introduced. By using indirect speech for the local man's first question, as well as the narrator's reply, the choice of indirect rather than direct dialogue seems indiscriminate, a matter simply of stylistic whim.

The tendency is perhaps not to notice consciously that throughout this exchange — and so many others in *Campos* — we have heard the narrator's voice pronounce only one word (he questions '¿Arena?' (16, 48) at one point in the conversation). Chapter 6 will contain a discussion of the first- and third-person forms ('yo' *versus* 'uno' and 'el viajero'), used by the narrator to refer to himself; at this point, let us merely note that these also play a part in the variations of distance between reader and narrator to be found in the text.

Aside from dialogue, the narrator's descriptions of people and places are equally significant in the shifting distances between us and him that they create. We have already seen in Chapter 3 how this affects the question of objectivity *versus* subjectivity, but it is worth mentioning here that this impinges on the question of how the narrator depicts himself. Sometimes the description, though grammatically couched in impersonal form, clearly represents a personal reaction, thus giving the reader a feeling of intimacy with the narrator's thoughts: 'El viajero tiene la impresión de recorrer una zona desértica, como las que se ven en las películas de vaqueros del oeste americano' (23, 56). At other times, he writes in the distant tones of a guide-book: 'Tres autobuses diarios cubren los nueve kilómetros de trayecto Almería-El Alquián. La carretera está alquitranada hasta Níjar y, a la salida de la ciudad, una bifurcación paralela a la nacional 340 lleva a los baños de Sierra Alhamilla' (15, 48). However, this register is rarely sustained for long; the sentence just quoted ends in a judgemental and therefore more confiding tone: 'en cuyo balneario, actualmente derruido, acostumbraban a reposar sus fatigas los ricos ociosos de la capital' (15, 48).

The problem of the narrator's identity, his distance from us, his proximity to Goytisolo, is inextricably bound up with the subject of the next chapter, fact versus fiction. If the text is seen unequivocally as non-fictional reportage then he has to be Goytisolo, since he calls himself 'yo' and Juan Goytisolo is printed on the title-page as the name of the writer. One might then wish to examine the issue of the unavoidable transformation of flesh-and-blood human being into literary personage, once he or she is used in a written text of any kind, but be that as it may, one could at least state with security that the narrator is Goytisolo, albeit a literary expression of him. However, if the text is at least in some respects fictional, then the 'yo' can be to some extent an invention, as in any story told in the first person.

The ambiguity of the narrator's relationship with the author is far from unique in Goytisolo's works. Many if not most of his protagonists share a greater or lesser number of experiences and opinions of the author, as one can easily see on reading his two volumes of memoirs, *Coto vedado* and *En los reinos de Taifa*. Álvaro Mendiola, hero of the trilogy of novels, *Señas de identidad*, *Reivindicación del conde don Julián*, and *Juan sin tierra*, is another character who is brought up in a bourgeois Barcelona family and leaves Spain to live in France as a young man. The protagonist of the later novel *Paisajes después de la batalla* (1982) actually resides at the same address as Goytisolo in Paris and is called 'goytisolo' (*sic*).

Perhaps the narrator of *Campos* could be seen as prefiguring the complexities of these later works to some extent. Although he may not be Goytisolo, he is close enough to him for the author to be able to portray him convincingly and without bad faith. If he has lived in the same places and has the same type of cultural baggage, the same moral and political attitudes as his author too, these can be represented all the more powerfully. This is surely why one of the most salient features of the text is that its narrator seems particularly credible and genuine. Ultimately, this is surely at the very heart of why the narrator, as Fussell asserted he must, is able to depict himself as likable: because, before all else, he rings true.

5. Fact and Fiction

Juan Goytisolo never went on the journey described in *Campos de Nijar*. To that extent, the work is a fiction. On the other hand, he has been, at different times, to all the places he describes. To that extent, the text is factual. This leaves us in an uncomfortably vague position: is *Campos* a novel, set in an area with which the author is well acquainted, or is it a non-fictional account with a little poetic licence in the condensation of several trips' itineraries into one? This chapter will seek to investigate the implications of these two ways of reading the text.

Would they affect the questions that we have considered in foregoing chapters: objectivity versus subjectivity and the identity of the narrator? Would they affect the socio-political criticism inherent in the work? Would they affect its value as literature?

Novels can create an illusion of objectivity, just as Goytisolo's own *La resaca*, written just before *Campos*, had attempted to do. And non-fictional documentary can be presented from a subjective point of view, as for example when a committed naturalist makes an impassioned television programme about the destruction of tropical rain forests. Thus the issue of subjectivity and objectivity need not interfere with the present discussion.

With the narrator's identity, the matter is more complex. It is true that people who exist as flesh-and-blood human beings are sometimes present in fiction, be they public figures like the Prime Minister, or celebrities like a film star or pop singer. Indeed one could conceive of a novel in which the narrator would be just such a person, the author having imagined how they would react to fictional circumstances invented for the novel. In one of Miguel de Unamuno's most famous works of fiction, *Niebla* (1914), the protagonist goes to visit Unamuno himself, in Salamanca, where the author really lived, and they have a discussion. As mentioned above, in one of Goytisolo's own fictional works, *Paisajes después de la batalla*, the protagonist is called goytisolo and lives at the author's address in Paris. Other examples could be found too, demonstrating that even if one chose to read the narrator as a literary representation of the author, that need not preclude the possibility of considering *Campos* a work of fiction.

However, on turning to the alternative approach to the text — that of viewing it as non-fiction — we are forced to narrow the field of possibilities. Then we cannot choose to read the narrator as a fictional construct: he will have to be Goytisolo, even though we may accept that this will be a literary version of him, analogous to the person who goes by the same name in his memoirs, *Coto vedado* and *En los reinos de Taifa*.

The presence and impact of socio-political criticism in *Campos de Níjar* need not be affected by its status as fact or fiction. Innumerable novels have powerfully criticized society, particular governments or laws, and this is not considered to interfere with their status as fiction. Finally, the value of the work as literature need not necessarily be affected by whether we classify it as fiction or fact, either. Collections of letters, and diaries, for example, are regularly evaluated for their literary merits, irrespective of their non-fictional status.

Thus, of the considerations that have been so far examined, only the position of the narrator is affected by the work's classification as fact or fiction. As we have seen, this is open to fewer readings if *Campos* is regarded as fact. But do we have a free choice in the matter? Can we simply decide to read it as one or the other or will textual and extra-textual evidence undermine our preference? It is true that it is impossible to prove that, for instance, a given conversation reported in the text did or did not take place, so one might argue that it is for the reader to elect whether to read it as a literary representation of words that were actually spoken to Juan Goytisolo on one of his trips to the South of Spain, or else an invention of the author reflecting his own feelings about the region. Ultimately, however, to speculate on such alternatives is futile.

Perhaps the most helpful way to deal with the problem is to do away with the concepts of fact and fiction as binary opposite terms. Instead, they could be imagined as a continuum which stretches between the maybe only theoretical extremes of pure fact and pure fiction, but which is mostly taken up by differently proportioned mixtures of the two. Then one could position the various types of discourse within *Campos* at different points along it. Let us consider an example:

> Entre el Cabo de Gata y Garrucha media una distancia de casi un centenar de kilómetros de costa árida y salvaje, batida por el viento en invierno, y por el sol y el calor en verano, tan asombrosamente bella como desconocida. Hay alcantilados, rocas, isletas, calas. La arena se escurre con suavidad entre los dedos y el mar azul invita continuamente al baño. (81, 96)

This paragraph, which opens Chapter 7 of *Campos de Níjar*, is a challenging mixture as far as subjectivity and objectivity are concerned, with value judgements slipped in amongst informative material. But where does it stand on the fact-fiction continuum? There seems to be little in it that could be called fiction in the normal usage of the term, but fact is sprinkled with opinion throughout. Nevertheless, perhaps because of this — ideas like 'asombrosamente bella' and the sensuous manner of describing the sand's quality instead of simply stating that it is fine and no more — the tone of the description is more in keeping with a novel than a non-fictional treatise. Hence, even if literal content would lead to the assertion that what we have here is fact and opinion, there is a novelistic element in that intangible feature of tone, which would justify placing the extract further towards fiction along the continuum than one might at first consider appropriate.

Here is quite another type of example:

> Mientras don Ambrosio sigue hablando de Castilla y el carácter noble y leal de sus paisanos, el coche se ciñe a las revueltas del camino, más allá del cortijo del

> Nazareno. El chófer fuma sin decir palabra y, de vez en
> cuando, me observa por el retrovisor. Los espartizales se
> barajan con los campos de trigo sobre la tierra ocre. De
> pronto llegamos a Los Nietos. (110, 113)

This is a piece of narrative rather than description, action rather than contemplation. Here the reader has a choice to make: either to believe that this records an incident that actually happened or to regard it as invention, a device to highlight a certain type of person, with certain stereotyped opinions. This would alter the position of the extract to some degree. Either way though, there can be little doubt that the passage is expressed in novelistic style. The narrator ranges around, pausing to describe now the driver, now the scenery outside. He skilfully conveys in this way how tedious Don Ambrosio's monologue is, for his failure to provide all but the basic import of it implies first, that it does not merit the effort of more exact transcription and second, that he himself is only half-listening to it anyway; looking out of the window and sizing up the driver are more interesting occupations. Here then is a passage which one could situate well towards the fiction end of the continuum, though not at its extremity: even if Don Ambrosio himself is an invention, his attitudes ring true and are, alas, typical of a certain variety of Spanish conservative. Incidentally, there are also the natural details of the crops and the colour of the soil, which push the passage a little further towards the fact end of the scale as well. Hence, we have a narrative technique that would befit a novel, but mixed with it some factual landscape description and a character who represents a real-life type even if he may be a fabrication.

One could make the same observation about all the people that the narrator encounters in *Campos de Níjar*. Whether or not they each bear the name and physical attributes of a specific individual whom Goytisolo has met on his travels in the area, they ring as true and typical as Don Ambrosio. However, one might argue that there is no difference between this and the characters in a realist novel. Dickens and Pérez Galdós, for example, both created hundreds of personages that ring true in all respects, as do many skilled contemporary novelists today, but nobody would try to use this as an argument for claiming that their works are not fiction. Writers in the realist tradition also can produce marvellously accurate and evocative descriptions of scenery that exists in real life, be it the backstreets of London or Madrid, be it rural beauty or neglect.

It therefore seems pointlessly stubborn, even churlish, to persist in classifying *Campos de Nijar* as non-fiction. Even if every character is based on a human being that Goytisolo has met in real life, the same could be said of many a character in a novel. One may say that the realism of the work is remarkably convincing and that this contributes to its documentary value, just as many of the novels of the 1950s in Spain, written by Goytisolo and his contemporaries, did; one may say that it is all true, in the artistic sense that it represents a true response in literary form to the author's real-life experience and opinions. But, how can one justifiably deny its fictional quality? Its finely balanced structure, its selectivity, its build-up to the climax of the storm in the weather and in the narrator's mood; all this and much more invite us to read it as a work of fiction.

Most critics take the sensible line of finding a comfortable position on the fence. Santos Sanz is unusual in treating the text as non-fiction and, moreover, in making no reference to the problematics of arriving at this reading (*12*, p.64). Even more damning and narrow is Paul Werrie's more or less contemporary (1965) judgement: he says that Goytisolo has turned 'au reportage, à l'enquête, au voyage, intérieur ou non, à l'exploration. [...] Et l'exploration ayant pour objet un monde où l'on meurt d'ennui ou de soleil, l'ouvrage ne saurait être sauvé que par la qualité de l'écriture à la manière d'un Cela', which, he implies, Goytisolo lacks.[18] Uncharacteristically, Michael Ugarte also appears to take this perhaps

---

[18] 'to reportage, to taking a survey, to the journey, interior or otherwise, to exploration. [...] And since the object of the exploration is a world where one dies of boredom or heatstroke, the work could only be saved by the high quality writing of a Cela.' Paul Werrie, 'Espagne: le cas de M. Juan Goytisolo', *La Table Ronde*, 204 (1965), 141–47 (p.143).

simplistic view: 'Assuming the role of a social scientist, Goytisolo travelled to the area on which he was to write, researched his subject, and documented his findings' (*16*, p.16).

Pablo Gil Casado, on the other hand, is more cautious when, citing the 'viejo de las tunas', he says: 'Es obvio que algunas de las personas que aparecen en estos relatos son el resultado de una transformación de la realidad, dándose así un personaje artísticamente elaborado, visto y sentido' (*2*, p.429). He takes a similar view when discussing Goytisolo's use of dialogue: 'Se trata de un lenguaje convencional, simplificado, que, excepto por algunas palabras regionales, es creación literaria' (*2*, p.433). Claudia Schaefer-Rodríguez non-committally alludes to the text as the 'literary result' of the author's travels in the area (*13*, p.160), and Kessel Schwartz finds an attractive compromise:

> Shots of life in process [...] create the impression of fiction. [...] If *Campos de Níjar* and the documentaries which follow it are not novels in the classic sense, neither are they travel books only. While his 'documentaries' contain some objective, almost photographic reproductions of the reality he is conveying, they also convert that reality, in all its desolation and dullness, into a novelistic and lyrical experience. [...] He creates in the reader's mind the feeling that he is reading a novel. (*14*, pp.117 and 121–22)

And Gonzalo Sobejano alludes to a 'realismo escueto', but adds that the travel books are 'no exentos, sin embargo, de rasgos novelescos'(*15*, p.361).

No critic of *Campos de Níjar* seems yet to have confronted directly the question which, to some degree, is a general one for literary criticism, but is especially pressing in the case of Juan Goytisolo's ambiguous works: where is the dividing-line between a novel based heavily on personal experience and a non-fictional memoir with its inevitable element of poetic licence? The answer has to be that there is no dividing-line at all; rather, the two meld imperceptibly into each other. *Campos de Níjar*, it could be asserted, resides precisely in this blurry crossover area.

This is a strength of Goytisolo's text, rather than an unfortunate feature. Let us note that the two critics who condemn the work (Sanz and Werrie) are precisely those who do not appreciate its complexity in this regard. By placing it in this uncertain area, the author can exploit the benefits of both fiction and non-fiction, as and when it suits his purpose. Thus, he can grant himself the freedom to doctor the itinerary of the journey so as to produce a suitably varied and artistically structured account; the meeting with Don Ambrosio, for example, comes at a point when the man's loathsome opinions will be very clearly revealed, without the narrator's needing to condemn them explicitly. Likewise, he can juggle with the types of comments heard from locals at different times and places and give them esthetic coherence, so that, for example, the drunken men at the beginning who sicken the narrator with their praise of Spain can be balanced by similar views expressed at the end:

>   —¡Qué mujeres!
>   —España es el mejó país del mundo.
>   —No tendrá el adelanto de otras naciones, pero pá
>   vivir...
>   —Caray, que no lo cambiaba yo por ninguno. (11, 47)

>   —El país es pobre, pero hermoso -decía el aperador.
>   —En España no hay el adelanto d'otras naciones, pero
>   se vive mejó que en ningún sitio -decía el azacán.
>   —Los extranjeros, en cuanto puén, se vienen p'aquí.
>   —En Andalucía, con el sol y un poquico de ná, se las
>   arregla usté y va tirando. (124, 123)

At the same time as making the most of this freedom to shape the material as a novelist can, Goytisolo also uses the non-fictional elements of the text with several effects. Sometimes they simply provide atmospheric descriptive background: 'Las casas son rectangulares, blancas' (71–72, 88). At other times, they provide historical or other scholarly material, which, as we have seen in the previous chapter, contributes to our respect for the narrator, as well as informing us interestingly: 'Entre Boca de los Frailes y San José había media docena de minas de plomo y manganeso. [...] Pero a primeros de siglo, las minas cerraron una tras otra' (85, 99).

Or finally, the non-fictional elements can be seen as literary devices of analogous effect to the range of techniques used by fiction writers to enhance the illusion of realism; ideas like starting a text with a statement explaining that the following pages were found by chance in the attic or that this is a story told by someone to the narrator and believed by him/her to be true; or else, the text may use footnotes and a scholarly style of discourse, as we find in Borges, for example. This sheds new light on the greater intimacy between narrator and reader observed at the beginning of *Campos de Níjar*. In addition to its effect on our view of the narrator, discussed above, it could be read as parallel to these age-old devices and designed, like them, to establish an illusion of non-fiction.

A further subtlety in Goytisolo's exploitation of both factual and fictional elements is to be found in the tightness with which he interweaves them. The comment on the lead and magnesium mines quoted above, for example, is presented, not as straightforward factual commentary from narrator direct to reader, but as part of a conversation with a colourful local character called Argimiro, who, to repeat, is a literary personage, whether or not he is based on someone whom the author has met. The result of this is that the factual truth of the content of what Argimiro tells the narrator spills over into the character himself, making him seem a non-fictional person, making the whole conversation, indeed, appear to be non-fiction.

Here is a different type of manifestation of the same technique:

El mozo trae un plato de bacalao con garbanzos y medio litro de vino. A diferencia del gaditano o malagueño, el

almeriense es poco aficionado a la bebida. La culpa se la
echo yo a los caldos del país, por lo general muy
medianejos. El que bebo ahora -vinagrón y algo
repuntado- difiere apenas del desbravado y zurraposo de
Garrucha. Sin poderlo evitar, me acuerdo con nostalgia
del tinto de Jumilla, que se encuentra a cien kilómetros
al norte -ligero, seco y deliciosamente áspero. (25, 59)

Instead of having factual information inextricably bound up with
novelistic dialogue as in the conversation about the mines, here it is
interwoven with narrative: the narrator's meal in the *fonda* of
Rodalquilar. Instead of presenting the information about local wines
and drinking-habits as just that — information, as one might find it
in a guide-book or wine encyclopedia — the narrator uses the
novelistic technique of having a sense experience spark off a train of
thought: it is the taste of the wine served to him that he presents as
the trigger for these reflections. Again, the effect is that in addition
to increasing our respect for the narrator owing to his knowledgeability and here, specifically, his discerning palate too, the factual
status of the information contained in the passage spills over into
the overall impact, so that the scene itself appears less fictionalized.

At times, the narrative of *Campos* is mixed not only with
factual information of the neutral kind that one might find, differently presented, in a guide-book, but also with socio-political
criticism. Let us consider one example of this three-way combination:

Me interno por las callejuelas laterales [al Paseo de
Níjar] en busca de los talleres de alfarería.
La cerámica de Níjar es famosa en todo el sur y, con
la de Bailén, una de las más importantes de España.
Barnizados y pintados de vivos colores, lebrillos y platos
se venden en Madrid, Barcelona y Valencia a precios
que sorprenderían sin duda a sus humildes autores.
(48, 72)

When the narrator later talks to some of the workers, it is confirmed that they make a wretched living from their pottery, because it is others who take the profits (49, 75). Here then we have narrative — the narrator's walk around Níjar — immediately followed by factual information — the status of the pottery from Níjar — and last, a comment that clearly implies that the potters are exploited. After the passage quoted comes description of their poor working conditions, and finally the conversation that reconfirms the narrator's comments above. The episode is crowned with a strong note of pathos, for the dialogue ends with the unfortunate workers saying how pleased they are to be potters, rather than miners (50, 76).

Here the narrative component strengthens the socio-political criticism, by making it seem less mediated by the narrator's personal convictions. The implication is that he visited Níjar and that this is a straightforward transcription of what he saw and heard, which has nothing to do with his own opinions. Were the same statement to be made without the framework of a travel narrative — if we simply read that the Níjar potters are unjustly exploited — it would be far easier to dismiss the comment as a reflection of a position in the political spectrum with which the reader may or may not sympathize. As part of a story, however, and backed by evidence of the narrator's knowledge of the ceramics industry in Spain, the commentary appears irrefutable. The narrative seems factual because it is accompanied by informative detail and the socio-political criticism appears to be straight description because of the influence of the narrative setting: all in all, a masterful use of the interweaving of fact, fiction, and comment.

Finally, let us consider the interweaving of narrative and socio-political criticism when it appears without the buffer of factual information. In the final chapter of *Campos de Níjar*, the narrator describes himself leafing through two conservative newspapers on the coach home:

> Mientras nos alejábamos del suburbio almeriense me
> entretenía hojeando las noticias: 'La selección española

> de baloncesto logra su séptima victoria consecutiva
> sobre la de Portugal', 'Primera Feria Regional de
> Actividades Leonesas', 'Desplazamiento de la
> alpargata...'.
>   La víspera me había pasado el día durmiendo y me
> sentía de nuevo en forma. (129, 125)

There is a strong though tacit critique here of the lack of press freedom. The triviality of the news items — the implication being that this inconsequential material is all that may be printed without incurring the censors' wrath — compared with the gravity of the Nijareños' plight gives a bitterly ironic flavour to the ending of the text. At the same time, the narrative is continuing; this is how the narrator is making his way north once more and this is what he did the previous day. Although the criticism is adequately conveyed — who could miss it? — it might be argued that it is rather less subtle here than in the rest of *Campos*. Perhaps this is because it contrasts so sharply with the other element of the passage, namely, the narrative thread. There is no spilling over of one into the other here, comparable to that which was observed when narrative and factual information plus socio-political criticism were interwoven; on one side we know that the narrator is sitting in a coach; on the other, we know that he is criticizing the Spanish press, but the two remain side by side rather than being powerfully fused.

However, the fact that this more overt style appears on the last page of the text is no doubt significant. One detects here a structural symmetry with the first chapter of *Campos*. There too, it will be recalled, the narrator was more open towards the reader about himself than elsewhere in the text. Now, at the end, he again opens his heart to us, though he reveals a different area of personal detail; it is not his childhood nor his youth in Barcelona now, but his concern with the printed word in Spain. On the level of social testimony, he registers the lamentable quality of the Spanish press; but perhaps by conveying this fact, he makes a literary point of even greater importance: he justifies why a novelist has written a travel book like *Campos* at all.

6. Language

The language of *Campos de Níjar* is likely to strike the reader as being lyrical without being pretentious in the descriptions, as evocative without being studied in the dialogues. These general characteristics are relatively obvious, even on first reading. However, there are other features of Goytisolo's use of language in the text that are less noticeable, but no less effective for that; these include his use of tenses, and the shifts between first- and third-person forms throughout the text, but there are also numerous individual turns of phrase that exert a powerful though quiet influence on the overall effect. A selection of these points, both the noticeable and the unobtrusive ones, the recurrent and the occasional, will be discussed in this chapter.

Chapter 3 has considered the lyricism of descriptive writing in *Campos* — in particular its imagery — in connection with the question of objectivity versus subjectivity. Let us turn first, therefore, to the other non-dialogue forms used in the text, namely the language of socio-political commentary, of historical and other background, and of narrative. Significantly perhaps, critics do not generally comment on the language of these components of the work, limiting themselves either to Goytisolo's evocation of landscape or the dialogue and analysing the content of the socio-political commentary and historical background rather than the language in which it is expressed. Little tends to be said of the narrative, except that it holds the work together logically.

One reason for this apparent gap in critical interest could be the unobtrusiveness of the language used in these domains. The words seem like a transparent vessel containing the meaning, making them difficult to notice, let alone to examine closely. However, this very feature is worthy of attention and has an important effect: it enables the reader to forget that the text is written by an individual with opinions and a personal perspective on the world, and it seems instead to comprise neutral information to be digested uncritically. The more noticeable the style of language is, the more readers are reminded that what they are reading has somebody's personal stamp on it; by the same token, the less one's attention is drawn to choice of words and sculpted syntax, the stronger the illusion of impersonal neutrality.

Let us consider an example of socio-political commentary in a passage briefly examined earlier in another context:

> 'La sierra es ocre, desértica. Su vegetación se reduce al palmito, que los almerienses emplean para fabricar escobas y esteras, y cuyo cogollo, blanco y sabroso, se consume, importado de Africa, en todos los países de Europa, donde es más estimado que el espárrago.
>
> (77, 94)

The implication of the comment is that if the Almerienses had access to the know-how and the wherewithal to process the palm hearts for export, the region would not be so impoverished. As it is, a potentially lucrative product is going to waste. Here is a simple informative sentence, the language of which seems quite unremarkable and yet there is an important nuance arising from the humble 'y' preceding 'cuyo cogollo'. If, instead of the 'y', the sentence read '*pero* cuyo cogollo', the comment would lose its light touch, becoming less subtle in its criticism. Added to that, the description of the palm hearts as 'blanco y sabroso', which is actually superfluous to the point being made, turns the knife in the wound, as it were, intensifying the pathos by sensuously evoking the product that the locals are squandering on brooms and mats.

A final ironic jab comes from the contrast between Europe, where the palm hearts are consumed, and Africa, where they are produced. Throughout *Campos*, the Níjar region is compared with Africa, with the implication that not only do they boast the same primitive beauty, but also that the area is as disadvantaged, climatically and financially, as that continent. Now we learn that Níjar is even more backward than Africa, for it does not even benefit from the few crops that it can cultivate in the difficult conditions. This vision of the region as inferior to Africa is thrown into even sharper relief by the mention of affluent Europe, where people can afford to buy delicacies imported from the other side of the world. Clearly, Níjar is not in Europe for the purposes of this sentence; nobody buys palm hearts there. Thus the region is isolated; it belongs nowhere — it is less developed than Africa (the resemblance to that continent is purely physical) — but it is also too poor to qualify for entry into Europe, continent of the wealthy consumer society.

Hence we have a sentence, unobtrusive in style but cunningly constructed; the juxtaposition of Europe and Africa, from both of which the region is excluded, has the effect of driving home the pathos of the Nijareños' plight, while the 'y' contributes to the illusion that the sentence is a cool and neutrally informative aside.

Not all of the non-descriptive, non-dialogue sections employ this type of technique, however. Sometimes the register is overtly emotive. Here, for example, is an extract from the narrator's thoughts on the history of Almería:

> Se me ocurre que los almerienses nunca han sido protagonistas de su historia, sino más bien comparsas, *resignados y mudos*. [...] Desde su conquista por los Reyes Católicos la región ha sufrido una ininterrumpida y *patética* decadencia. [...] Los almerienses *regaron con su sangre* las posesiones de Europa, África, Oceanía y América. [...] En el siglo XVIII era ya *la cenicienta* de nuestras provincias. [...] Continuó *ofrendando* sus hijos al país. [...] Formaron la callada tripulación de los galeones, la sufrida tropa de los ejércitos, la mano de obra *oscura y abnegada*. [...] Las fosas comunes del mundo entero contienen sin duda un buen porcentaje de almerienses. (109–10, 112–13; my italics)

The italicized words and phrases are no doubt the most striking for their emotional charge, but the whole passage is written in melodramatic tones. To make mention of such celebrated examples of hardship as the galleons, or such quintessential emblems of wretchedness as paupers' mass graves, has at least as powerful an effect as to use adjectives like 'abnegada'.

Here, as it were, the narrator plays straight with the reader. The language makes it abundantly clear that he is deeply moved by the history of Almería and is giving a version of it from that self-declared position. There is a danger, therefore, that one might choose to dismiss his version as sensationalized and too coloured by emotion to remain reliable, something that is a far less likely reaction to the explanation about the palm hearts, where the language was used to build an illusion of neutrality. However, the risk is a well calculated one, for several reasons. First, the historical facts embedded in the emotion are accurate and can be verified in reference works. Second, what may be lost in persuasive power over the readers is balanced by the gain in their sympathy and respect for the narrator as an individual. How can one not warm to someone who takes so much to heart the plight of anonymous people who have been unjustly treated down the centuries? As we saw in Chapter 4, it is important for the narrator to be a likable character; here he wins much on that score, even if he risks losing some persuasive power by this relinquishing of apparent neutrality.

Let us now consider the way in which language is used in the narrative of *Campos de Níjar*. Does Goytisolo tend to the apparent transparency of the palm hearts style or the open sentiment of the history quotation, or is another type of language altogether called into play? This is the opening of Chapter 5:

> Había dicho a la patrona que me despertase de alborada
> con el sano propósito de ver despuntar el sol sobre la
> sierra, pero las sábanas se me pegaron más de lo debido.
> Los felices trabajadores en domicilio hemos abandonado
> la costumbre de madrugar para ganar el pan y el autor
> de estas líneas se levanta a la hora en que el guadapero
> lleva el serillo del almuerzo a los segadores. (55, 78)

There is indeed a new element in this style, namely, familiarity verging on the colloquial. Not only is this passage noticeable for its use of the mildly humorous set expression 'pegársele a uno las sábanas', but what it actually is saying is more personal than one might expect, compared with the passages quoted earlier. Almost as in the tone of Chapter 1, here the narrator confides his sleeping habits to the reader and even goes so far as to offer an explanation for why he finds it difficult to rise early, which causes him to refer to his lifestyle when he is not travelling in southern Spain. Again one may note a sympathy-winning effect, here arising from the fact that he is prepared to reveal such details of his private life. This establishes a flattering sense of intimacy reminiscent of the historical passage for the common willingness to expose clearly personal information.

The self-deprecating tone, whereby the narrator implies that his habit of rising late is unhealthy, and that in this respect he is inferior to farm labourers, may at first seem equally endearing, but it soon transpires that the apparently self-directed disapproval was in fact nothing of the kind. A few lines later we learn that the narrator is not really contrite for having overslept, but rather is playfully mocking the innkeeper's attitude to this. She is 'escandalizada' and views him as 'perezoso' with her 'mirada desaprobadora', while he cheerfully checks out and goes to the barber (55, 78).

Thus the extract is only deceptively straightforward, for it masks a complex transfer of point of view, such that the narrator portrays himself as he imagines the innkeeper sees him, but without ever explicitly explaining that this is what he is doing. To this degree, the importance of implicit nuance is analogous to the palm hearts passage, where, too, one reading would not reveal its subtlety.

On proceeding to consider the use of dialogue in *Campos de Níjar*, we find that several critics have something to say about it and especially about Goytisolo's use of phonetically transcribed dialect forms of pronunciation, but there is no general consensus. Pablo Gil Casado asserts: 'Se trata de un lenguaje convencional, simplificado, que, excepto por algunas palabras regionales, es creación literaria' (2, p.433). Gonzalo Navajas, on the other hand, appears to see the author's hand as being virtually absent apart from his task as transcriber: 'Es el transmisor que nos comunica los puntos de vista de los habitantes de Almería con los que conversó [...] y que cumplen en el libro un papel de interlocutores-informantes', adding a general comment on all of Goytisolo's travel works:

> Se nota en ellos un esfuerzo constante por reproducir el lenguaje popular coloquial. [...] Con este procedimiento, Goytisolo pretende reintroducir el habla popular dentro de la literatura de posguerra. Más que una pretensión pintoresca se trata de un propósito documental. (*9*, pp.118 and 119).

In Peter Bush's introduction to the Tamesis Texts edition, he appears to consider that Goytisolo has partially failed in his portrayal of local Spanish:

> Goytisolo reproduces the commonest aspects of the southern register and this was a clear necessity for the sake of authenticity. [...] However, there is no more than a flavour of the southern register. [...] There are some inconsistencies and far too many non-dropped 's'es. The total lack of swearing is also striking. (p.33)

Gil Casado, on the other hand, sees the author's selectivity with dialect forms as a wise literary choice: 'El escritor no puede reproducirla [la lengua rural] constantemente a lo largo de la obra, pues perjudicaría la calidad literaria' (*2*, p.434).

It would seem somewhat presumptuous for critics to feel they can know what the author was trying to achieve and therefore be in a position to assert that the attempt is successful or otherwise. Let us therefore limit ourselves to determining what Goytisolo's use of dialogue does achieve, the effects it does have, without venturing into conjecture about authorial intentions.

It is quite true that a phonetician who went to Almería to conduct research on the local dialect would almost certainly produce transcriptions of dialogue very different from those we find in *Campos de Níjar*. On the other hand, it seems unreasonable to regard this as proof that Goytisolo's dialogue is flawed, given that his work is literary rather than a piece of linguistic research. Even on the simplistic level of accuracy, however, it is perhaps worth noting that different individuals in the same geographical area have a variety of accents, as gender, class, and age all have their influence along with region. Another factor is that when speaking to an outsider, some but not all people will attempt to speak in a more standard form. It could therefore be argued that if the thickness of the dialect alters from one speaker to another in *Campos*, this may not be only poetic license, but might be seen as a realistic reflection of the well-attested non-uniformity in any given dialect.

We have already noted, in discussing the narrator's position, how little he records his own words in direct speech, relative to those of his interlocutors, thus creating an atmosphere imbued with Andalusian rhythms and an illusion of minimal or even non-existent mediation on his part. Let us now look more closely at a sample extract of such dialogue. When the narrator is invited into a house in Níjar and introduced to his host's wife and children, there is an exchange concerning the baby's blindness that runs as follows:

> Modesta se adelanta a mi pensamiento:
> —Lástima que sea cieguico.
> —No ve ná — dice el hombre —. Está asín desde que
>   nació.
> Les pregunto si lo ha visitado algún médico.
> —A Almería lo llevaron una vez. Dijeron que tendrían
>   que operarle.
> —¿Allí?
> —No. En Barcelona.
> —Parece que en Barcelona hay un médico mú bueno.
> —Bueno o malo, pá nosotros es iguá.
> —No sé por qué dices eso -se lamenta la mujer.
> —Porque es verdá. Como no encontramos naide que nos
>   fíe el viaje... (45, 70–71)

The Andalusian pronunciation of this couple is relatively strong, although it remains easy to decipher what they are saying and the accent is not transcribed at every opportunity, for the 's' of 'lástima' and the 'z' of 'vez' are allowed to stand, for example. There is the classic switch to indirect speech for the narrator's contribution to the conversation, except for the occasional word, like the '¿Allí?' question here. The content of the conversation is typical of the whole of *Campos* too, with its recurrent depiction of appalling deprivation here taking the form of lack of medical facilities, though with the added pathos of the victim's being a helpless, unnecessarily blind baby. The other ubiquitous theme of the text also emerges in this fragment: namely the locals' vision of Barcelona and Catalonia in general as a utopia, although here, for once, we see a concrete reason for the status of the city in the minds of these southerners, rather than a sad half-true fantasy based on hearsay.

To hear the voices of people in such pathetic circumstances, rather than simply to be told, however forcefully, that the medical services in the area are totally inadequate, has a far more powerful effect on the reader, for two main reasons. First, the fact of meeting individuals, with voices and speech idiosyncrasies, gives the problem an immediacy impossible to create from statistical data or even from emotive explanation similar to that which was used when the narrator was commenting on the history of the region. Second, by building the illusion of non-mediation by the narrator, through the use of direct speech and minimal intervention on his part, it is harder to dismiss the case as a biased presentation of the situation. On reflection, of course, this is just as arguable for dialogue as for narrative discourse, since both have been written by Juan Goytisolo, but in terms of irrational gut reaction, this strikes the reader as more irrefutable proof of the locals' plight than to be told of it indirectly.

Thus the presentation of deprivation through dialogue creates an illusion of unvarnished, unbiased truth, and the presentation of dialogue in dialect gives the speakers greater individuality, thus plausibility, thus pathos, as well as complementing the illusion of the narrator as recorder rather than creator of text.

The illusion is further enhanced by the inclusion in *Campos* of some dialogue which the narrator clearly finds irritating, even sickening. I have already considered Don Ambrosio's opinions and have cited dialogue at the beginning and the end of the text in which local people sing the praises of their country, equally distasteful to a narrator clearly in despair with it. This material, together with a certain amount of inconsequential talk, helps to give an impression of indiscriminate recording of what was said, rather than careful selection of what the narrator finds most pertinent to the picture he wishes to paint.

In the comments that are interspersed with passages of conversation, the tense most frequently found is the present, as we see in the 'adelanta' and 'pregunto' of the example quoted above. This is another factor in creating immediacy, along with the presence of direct speech itself. Even when the non-dialogue insertions become descriptive rather than explanatory of who is speaking, the present remains the tense most commonly found: 'Mientras seguimos de palique, la carretera atraviesa unos olivares. [...] Se advierte la proximidad de un pueblo y, un centenar de metros más lejos, llegamos a la carretera comarcal' (40, 68).

Indeed, if one counted how many verbs were in each tense in *Campos de Níjar*, there can be little doubt that the present would romp to victory, for not only are the passages of dialogue with their insertions written almost exclusively in the present, nearly all the landscape description is too: 'Níjar se incrusta en los estribos de la sierra y sus casas parecen retener la luz del sol' (43, 69). As well as immediacy, an effect of this usage is to make the descriptions seem universal, not limited to an impression formed by one individual — the narrator — at a particular moment on a particular journey, but somehow generally true, so that anyone who saw the same view at any time would describe it likewise. This is a pleasant feature for those who like to be the classic readers of travel works: the armchair travellers who enjoy imagining themselves in the narrator's shoes.

Even descriptions of action persist in using the present tense: 'Por la calle bajan mujeres vestidas de negro y un gitano sentado a horcajadas sobre un borrico' (43, 69). This makes the women as timeless as the scenery, part of it indeed, for the implication is that as well as finding the houses of Níjar looking the same at any time, it is equally true that whenever anyone goes to Níjar there will be women in black and a token gypsy to be seen in the street. One can simply read this as the historic present, the device for telling a story with maximum immediacy and vividness, but without denying this, it would seem that it also helps create an atmosphere of changelessness.

In fact, the more usual narrative past tenses are only to be found consistently in the first and last two chapters of *Campos de Níjar*, which, as we have already seen, differ from the rest of the text in other ways too. By having them in a different tense from the main body of the text, there is an effect analogous to switching from black and white to colour in a film. Suddenly, the narrative leaps into vividness, immediacy, three dimensions after the nostalgic calm of Chapter 1's memories of the area. The same happens in reverse at the end of the work. After reaching a climax of emotional charge at the end of Chapter 9, coinciding with the desperate young man begging an embarrassed and guilt-ridden narrator to help him leave the region, the text withdraws to the cool distance of the past tense and the beginning of the homeward journey.

This creates a grammatical symmetry in *Campos* to match its narrative pattern of framing the text in arrival at and departure from the region, and in addition to the further symmetry of content with the two conversations echoing each other and a mood of despairing love permeating the narrator's tone.

A similar — though not identical — phenomenon is to be found on consideration of the text's fluctuation between first- and third-person discourse. Whilst the first-person singular is certainly in evidence throughout *Campos de Níjar*, it is only in the main body of the text (Chapters 2 to 9 inclusive) that the various third-person alternatives to refer to the narrator are utilized. Here are a few examples:

> Junto al henequén y el nopal, el viajero encuentra otra
> planta. [...] Con vistas a la obtención de caucho, el
> Instituto inició hace tiempo su cultivo. [...] A juzgar por

la opinión de quienes he interrogado, no parece que [...]
el éxito haya recompensado sus esfuerzos. (18, 50)

Uno piensa que lo sucedido hace dos siglos en Níjar es
hoy por hoy moneda corriente en el país. (51–52, 77)

El propio caminante — que, desde que vive en el norte,
se ahila y desmedra como las plantas privadas de luz y
es un apasionado del sol — siente el agobio del trayecto
y empieza a buscar un trocito de sombra donde
tumbarse.

No hay ninguno y continúo todavía un buen rato.
(57, 79)

As the first and third of the above examples show, these alternative
forms are freely mixed with the straightforward first-person singular. There is also a great deal of use for the first-person plural in the
text, as soon as the narrator has a companion. Are these alternative
forms merely providers of variety, just stylish substitutes for saying
'yo'? Although they do offer relief from the first-person singular, it
would seem that they alter the distance between narrator and reader
as well, with two main consequences regarding degrees of intimacy
on the one hand and universality on the other.

The use of 'el viajero' in the first example is surely more
distant than 'yo' would have been, a distance soon shortened again
by the rapid return to the first-person singular of 'he interrogado'.
Until we reach that 'yo'-form, however, the impression is not only
impersonally distant, a negative point perhaps, but also has the
counterbalancing positive feature of implying universality, so that
readers who enjoy armchair travelling can visualize themselves as
being that 'viajero' and making the same observation. Thus, by
using the form of 'el viajero', the narrator creates an image of
himself as everyman-traveller, reinforcing the illusion of neutrality
as well as entertainingly inviting us to identify with him.

The 'uno' form of the second example feels much closer to the
first-person singular than 'el viajero' did, in much the same way
that 'one' is used self-referentially by certain speakers of English

(though without the upper-class stigma attached to the form in Britain). Nevertheless, it does contribute something to the everyman-traveller effect of neutrality, implying — albeit more faintly than in the use of 'el viajero' — that anyone faced with the same spectacle would think as the narrator did.

The final example seems to be a case of finding an alternative to 'yo' for the sake of stylistic elegance. If 'caminante' had appeared unqualified, it would have been parallel to the usage of 'el viajero', providing the same distance and everyman quality, but the fact that it is supported by the adjective 'propio' means that it cannot be taken as a statement applying to any 'caminante', a suspicion confirmed immediately afterwards by the reference to the narrator's personal tolerance of hot weather, followed by the swift return to the first-person singular.

Thus it is clear that each of these third-person forms must be considered on its own merits; the range of implications varies, as we have seen, not only with the particular words chosen — 'viajero' versus 'uno' versus 'caminante' — but also with the context: the qualifying 'propio', the way in which the discourse returns to the first person or provides unequivocally personal information.

The language of *Campos de Níjar* is a skilful blend of apparent — but only apparent — neutrality, universality, transparency, with open commitment and emotional involvement by the narrator. Paradoxically, the fact that he does declare his position on occasions such as his account of the history of the region reinforces rather than undermines the illusion of reliability and neutrality elsewhere, for it creates an impression of moral integrity and openness on the narrator's part that makes the reader swallow what he presents in neutral tones simply as information. The balance is a fine one, masterfully negotiated by Juan Goytisolo and surely the first real foretaste of the major works he would start producing later in the 1960s.

7. Conclusion

La Chanca, published two years after *Campos de Níjar*, is also a travel work about the South of Spain and for that reason a better understanding of the author's approach to the area, and to the kind of writing that he deems appropriate to evoke it, can be gained by comparing and contrasting the two texts; in this way, we should discover what is unique to the earlier travel work as well as glimpse the direction in which Goytisolo moved after the literary turning-point which it marked.

Critics often lump the two works together despite their many differences. Exceptions are Santos Sanz and Jesús Lázaro. Sanz controversially asserts that 'en *La Chanca* hay algo más de construcción artística que en *Campos de Níjar*' (*12*, p.65), perhaps because of the more developed story-line. Lázaro also prefers the second work, but for different — though equally debatable — reasons:

> Juan Goytisolo anula en esta obra el pintoresquismo existente en la obra anterior, *Campos de Níjar*. [...] El hombre se convierte en el centro de la obra, no es uno más de sus componentes. [... Hay en *La Chanca*] el abandono del falso objetivismo presente en *Campos de Níjar*. [...] El cambio de perspectiva posibilita un mayor acercamiento afectivo a la realidad y una más intensa comunión con los individuos. (*7*, pp.11–12)

On the whole *La Chanca* is made of stronger stuff than *Campos de Níjar*. Perhaps because it deals exclusively with urban poverty, there are far fewer breathing-spaces in which to contemplate the beauty of natural surroundings. Moreover, the political protest element is more direct (*9*, p.120), since the premise for the journey to La

Chanca is the narrator's search for a particular man whom he has been asked, by the man's cousin in Paris, to look up. But it transpires that the man was taken away by the authorities some days previously, leaving his family angry, frightened, and completely ignorant of what will happen, when and whether they will see him again.

Perhaps the first development that one notices in the later work is the more obtrusive personal dimension. As we saw in Chapter 4 of this Guide, the narrator of *Campos* minimizes the personal information he provides, so that the first and last chapters (and the occasional moment in between) stand out because of their exceptionally intimate tone relative to the majority of the text. *La Chanca*'s narrator, on the other hand, begins by associating himself with Juan Goytisolo more closely, giving details of his life in Paris and nostalgia for Spain, so that although we are still dealing with a guide who is a literary figure, this is more unequivocally than in *Campos* a literary version of the author.

The narrator of the later work also depicts himself as more uncomfortable in the company of those he meets, because of his vastly privileged position in the social hierarchy compared with theirs. There are moments in *Campos*, to be sure, when the narrator squirms with guilt and embarrassment at his social superiority, when he cannot sleep for thinking of it (52, 77); and when he leaves behind Juan, the man who has begged him to help him go to Catalonia (117, 120). However, these episodes stand out precisely because, for most of the text, the narrator does not seem to feel that he is intruding voyeuristically into the lives of people less fortunate than himself; on the contrary, he often describes scenes in which he appears to mix with a group of locals unproblematically, as for example when he accepts a ride in a lorry with workers from the gold mine and they chat happily for the duration of the journey on subjects ranging from different ways of cooking lizard in northern and southern Spain, to the problems of a man suffering from silicosis (32–36, 63–65).

In *La Chanca*, by contrast, the narrator seems more painfully aware of his status as an outsider and possibly an intruder.[19] He often refers to himself not as 'el viajero' as in the earlier work, but, significantly, as 'el forastero'; moreover, when he first enters the neighbourhood, he sees himself as if from without, and in striking contrast to the narrator's non-visibility to the reader in *Campos* he depicts himself as 'vestido, calzado, defendiéndose de la acometida del sol con unas gafas ahumadas' (*LCh*, p.27), which brings him to 'la conciencia de estar allí de más' (*LCh*, p.28). Reflecting this ability to see himself, we hear his voice more than in *Campos* too; the device of reproducing the locals' words in direct speech and his own in indirect form is used more sparingly in the second work. Compare, for example, the following snatches of dialogue. The first, from *Campos*, occurs when a group of children show the narrator the Paseo of Níjar; the second, from *La Chanca*, when the narrator finally locates the family of the man whose cousin he met in Paris.

> —Lo inauguraron [el Paseo] el año pasao — dice Antoñico —. ¿Qué le parece?
> La chiquillería está al acecho de mis palabras y digo que me parece muy bien.
> —De noche lo iluminan y tó.
> —Debe quedar muy bonito.
> —Mucho. Venga de aquí a dos horas y lo verá. [...]
> —¿Qué quié vé usté más?
> Doy las gracias a Antoñico por sus amabilidades y le digo que me voy a la posada. (47–48, 72)

Here, only one out of the three things the narrator says is reproduced in direct form, whereas indirect form is not used at all for the children.

> —Perdone — digo —. ¿Vive aquí uno que llaman Antonio Roa el Cartagenero? [...]

---

[19] See Prefatory Note for publication details. References will be given in the text, using the abbreviation *LCh*.

—Sí señó. Ésta es su casa.

—¿Podría hablar con él un momento? […]

—¿Pa qué lo busca usté?

—Soy un amigo de su primo, el Vitorino…

—Mi marío no está.

—¿Cuándo vuelve? […]

—¿Decía usté que es amigo de Vitorino?

—Sí señor. Nos conocimos en París y, al saber que yo
venía por aquí, me dio una tarjeta con su dirección.
(*LCh*, pp.41–42)

Just as we are allowed to see the visual contrast between the locals
and the narrator in *La Chanca*, the above extract shows how the
narrator permits the aural contrast to be conveyed too, by letting the
narrator's standard Spanish appear alongside the local dialect.

One of the effects of this greater prominence given to the
contrasting of the narrator with the locals is that he — and therefore
we — feel uncomfortable at his invasion of the locals' lives. At one
point, for instance, he mentions that one of his guides 'parece
contento de despedirse de mí' (*LCh*, p.34), whereas in *Campos* all
the locals seemed delighted to spend time with the narrator. Even
with the family of the missing man, who make the narrator
welcome, he seems concerned not to overstay his welcome: 'Yo no
quería venir por no molestarles, pero el Luiso ha insistido' (*LCh*,
p.72). Compare this delicacy with the insouciant approach of the
narrator of *Campos* in similar circumstances: when he visits the
family with the blind baby in Níjar, it never seems to occur to him
that he might be imposing and when he leaves, this is described
only in terms of his own desire to extricate himself:

> Yo aprovecho la ocasión para levantarme.
> —Su compañía es muy grata, pero oscurece, y quisiera
> dar una vuelta por el pueblo. (46, 71)

Thus the narrator of *Campos* can be seen to be somewhat insensitive, or perhaps naïve, in comparison with his counterpart in *La*

Chanca, with respect to his apparent belief that he can fit in unprob-lematically with the locals most of the time. This is an element of his character that might well pass unnoticed were it not for the sharp contrast afforded by the later work. The difference is exemplified most powerfully perhaps in the fact that in *Campos* the narrator cannot or will not see himself from the outside, as he appears to the Nijareños, whereas in *La Chanca* there is the memorable self-portrait of the smart 'forastero' with his sunglasses walking past 'los grupos de mujeres, viejos y chiquillos que hozan y merodean por los escombros' (*LCh*, p.27).

The second travel work is structured around a stronger story-line than *Campos* had with its simple premise of three days in the Níjar area and no specific goal in mind. Here we have an account of the narrator's meeting someone from La Chanca in Paris and then setting out to find his family, followed by the intrigue concerning the disappearance of the cousin, and ending with nothing resolved but a drunken night's sleep in his family's home and the dawn of a new day. However, whilst this may seem to orient the work more in the direction of a short novel than a documentary work, any such impression is counteracted by the extensive documentary material (*6*, p.261), which here, in contrast to its treatment in the earlier work, makes no attempt to justify its inclusion by means of present-ing itself as something brought to the narrator's mind by his circumstances. There is no need for *La Chanca*'s 'forastero' to depict himself ordering some wine in an inn so as to have a reason for giving an opinion on local wines and drinking-habits, no need for him to meet a Don Ambrosio in order to muse over the attitudes of non-Andalusian Spaniards towards the region over the centuries. There is no need because Goytisolo appends most of his documen-tary material in a separate section after the ending of the narrator's account of his own trip to La Chanca. This consists of selections from writings about the area dating back to the twelfth century and some statistics concerning the depopulation of the region. The effect of these appendices is retrospectively to reinforce the impression of impartial truth in the personal depiction of La Chanca given in the narrative section of the text, though, as we saw in the case of dialogue and photographs in *Campos de Níjar*, the fact that these are the extracts selected by the author to support his case makes this no more than an impression. Particularly effective is the Madrid newspaper clipping that gives a description of La Chanca contrary to that which we have been reading, seeing it as '*el más pintoresco barrio de pescadores del mundo*' (*LCh*, p.124; journalist's italics). This achieves two ends: first, it suggests that the passages have not been selected because they agree with Goytisolo's point of view, thus creating an illusion of indiscriminateness, of even-handed neutrality. Second, by reproducing this positive vision of a place where we have been reading about undeserved and unremitting human misery, hardship, and despair, it constitutes a damning indictment of the type of journalism that prettifies instead of offering its readers the unpalatable truth. Another consequence of incorporating chunks of other people's writings is highlighted by Michael Ugarte:

> It is the first hint of a linguistic attack on 'la España oficial',[20] an attempt to mesh the social criticism of the regime with a critique of that regime's language.
> Behind the voices of the writers of the official descriptions of La Chanca is the ironic authorial voice of Goytisolo. (*16*, p.18)

On one occasion, there is an extended version of the method of introducing documentary material found in *Campos de Níjar*. Chapter 9 of *La Chanca* opens with a page and a half of historical background, complete with quotations from scholars, dates, and other researched facts. Unintroduced, it appears at first to be simply an interlude with no premise for being there, but then, to the reader's surprise and probably incredulity, the following paragraph implies that these are supposed to have been the narrator's thoughts:

---

[20] This is arguable, since official language had already come under fire in *La resaca*, with one of the characters objecting to the falsity of language in Franco's Spain, much as we find in Luciano's comments in *La Chanca*, p.89. See *6*, p.263.

'El Luiso camina junto a mí ensimismado y, *como si hubiera adivinado mis pensamientos*, me coge del brazo y me mira de hito en hito a los ojos' (*LCh*, p.67; my italics). The artificiality of the device undermines the status of the narrative as non-fiction, despite the close association of narrator with author. Consequently, it reinforces one's sense that the narrative is an excuse for the documentary, testimonial element, rather than an equal partner coexisting happily at its side.

Hence, by including more overt documentary material than *Campos* did, but by also having a stronger story-line and by identifying the narrator with the author more unequivocally, *La Chanca* brings together elements more disparate than the earlier work with its less ambitious combination of mildly fictional, mildly autobiographical, and mildly factual material. Where in *Campos*, as the previous chapters of this study have shown, boundaries were subtly blurred — between objectivity and subjectivity, between neutrality and ideological commitment, between fiction and memoir and fact — here they are sharply delineated and all pull in different directions, leaving readers with the impression that they have read not one but three texts: an episode from Goytisolo's autobiography at the beginning, with the account of the narrator's feelings towards Spain while living in Paris; a short story in the social realist style about a poor man taken away by the authorities and his family; and a work of non-fiction about Almería's history, geography, sociology, and depiction by writers down the centuries.

Which type of approach is to be preferred can only depend on personal taste, but the contrast between the works in this respect serves to highlight the author's skill in *Campos de Níjar*, where the same components are blended so smoothly that it is with difficulty and only partial success that a critic can prise them apart.

Having considered some of the principal divergences in Goytisolo's treatment of travel writing in *Campos de Níjar* and *La Chanca*, let us now turn to consider some of the features that remain constant or undergo only complementary variations on passing from one text to the other. One is the attitude of a certain type of *machista* Andalusian, which enters *Campos de Níjar* relatively mildly in Chapter 1, when some girls pass by dressed up for a christening. First 'un hombre las piropeó con voz ronca' (11, 46) and then one of the drunken men in the bar that the narrator enters exclaims '¡Qué mujeres!' (11, 47), sparking the brief exchange with his companion about Spain being the best country in the world. The narrator's reaction to this is understated though no less clear for that; he avoids joining them when they invite him to do so and he describes them unflatteringly as resembling 'dos pajarracos montaraces' (11, 47).

   In *La Chanca*, a similar group of men is encountered, but the description is longer and far more odious, and the narrator's reaction this time is to voice his disgust, albeit to someone who does not understand what he means. Rather than admiring — however coarsely — some passing girls, these men are complaining about the female talent in Almería, each using the conversation to brag about his exploits with women from other regions. They complain indignantly about the high prices charged by prostitutes and share tips on how to avoid paying the full amount. The narrator makes no secret of his loathing for this type of attitude, asking a young woman collecting for cancer research, 'cuándo había colecta para combatir el Gran Cáncer' (*LCh*, p.19).

   Here, then, we find a theme that appeared in mild form in *Campos* developed and reinforced in *La Chanca*. A similar pattern is to be found with the subject of foreign visitors. As we have seen, the narrator's attitude in the first of the Andalusian travel works is somewhat ambivalent: he makes fun of the French tourists in their Peugeot and gives an extremely negative picture of the American fleet, but the Swedes seem to be just harmless eccentrics and there is even a note of regret that tourism is not more highly developed in such a beautiful region and where the money it would earn is so desperately needed. There is far less ambivalence in *La Chanca*, for here tourists are given a much less tempered negative weighting. In summary, they are depicted as exploitative and aggressively voyeuristic or as simply stupid and unadventurous. The first variety is characterized by the group of French visitors to La Chanca who had taken pleasure in photographing scenes of poverty. We hear of them through the mother of the missing man, for she and her grand-children had been one of their subjects. It is clear that what interested the visitors was the sordidness of the place and its living conditions:

> —Llevaban un aparatico asín de pequeño y nos echaron más de cien retratos. Yo quería que mis nietos se arreglaran un poquico, pero ellos dijeron que no, que ya estaban bien... Los tres parecían unos gitanos.
> —Mi Candelín iba desnudo -dice Pepe. (*LCh*, p.48)

Luiso perceives the behaviour of the French as offensive even though he probably misinterprets their reasons for wanting to photograph naked children:

> —Si llego a está yo les fuera obligao a quitarse la ropa a ellos — dice el Luiso —. Los tíos guarros. (*LCh*, p.48)

In a similar vein, though far less obtrusively, the verb used by the narrator to refer to tourists who take photographs of Almería from the Alcazaba is 'acribillar' (*LCh*, p.21).

The other type of tourist mentioned is the incurious group that simply heads for the Málaga coast without stopping to explore a district like La Chanca which lies off the main road (*LCh*, p.27), or the sightseers who silently listen to the ridiculous commentary of their Gibraltarian guide (*LCh*, p.21).

The French photographers could perhaps be seen as the development of the French tourists in *Campos*; the kind of rich travellers who deliberately choose what they see as a primitive place for their holiday destination, because they want to observe primitive people and their lifestyle. In *Campos* they were ridiculous; by *La Chanca* they have become offensively voyeuristic, treating the locals as if they were freaks. The eccentrics like the Swedes of *Campos* have faded out of the picture as have the American sailors (in *La Chanca*, the Americans are doling out milk to the poor, so at least are depicted as charitable, albeit in a patronizing way).

The foolish tourists interested only in the beach are perhaps precisely those that the narrator felt ought to be attracted to the Nijareño coastline; although little is said about them, this limited amount is not flattering:

> Las casas situadas en primer término ocultan púdicamente a los turistas que se dirigen por carretera a la costa de Málaga la existencia de un barrio insólito [La Chanca. ...] Por regla general, los automovilistas prosiguen su camino sin pararse a indagar lo que hay detrás. (*LCh*, p.27)

In later works, tourists will be lambasted pitilessly, but in this movement from *Campos de Níjar* to *La Chanca* the downhill progression is already perceptibly underway. The Spanish tourist boom only took off in the 1960s, so it is logical that in the works written up to and including *Campos de Níjar*, published in 1960, foreign visitors either are absent or do not evoke strong feelings. It is from *La Chanca* (1962) onwards that the resentment towards the invasive hordes of holidaymakers will really set in.

Despite the fact that there are no beautiful rural landscapes to describe in *La Chanca*, it is not a dull work in terms of evocative language. There are many sensuous effects, ranging from 'el tacto amistoso, velludo' of Vitorino's hand when he and the narrator reminisce about Almería together in Paris (*LCh*, p.10) to the sinister description of nightfall in La Chanca:

> Al oscurecer, es una guarida de lobos. Las luces del alumbrado público se espacian peligrosamente a medida que uno trepa por la ladera y el silencio es tan fuerte, contiene en su interior tanta amenaza, que vibra y zumba en el aire, lo mismo que un sonido. (*LCh*, p.93)

The changing strength of the sunlight and its effects on colour are sensitively recorded too: 'El sol ha comenzado a bajar poco a poco y parece que se respira mejor. La luz respeta la variedad de los matices. Las casas ya no son uniformemente blancas y el azul del cielo se intensifica' (*LCh*, p.59). We are not spared the mixture of smells — bleach, disinfectant, and refuse — either. So even if the subject-matter in this second work cannot boast the savage beauty of the scenery in the first, Goytisolo accords it equal respect in using his skills as a writer to portray the scenes of urban deprivation as vividly as the mountains and fields of Níjar.

*

We have seen how different types of discourse mingle in *Campos de Níjar*, and by way of comparison we have briefly looked at an alternative, more clear-cut approach in *La Chanca*. In conclusion, it is worthwhile to consider the extent to which the different elements in *Campos* undercut or complement each other.

Perhaps it is inadvisable in the final analysis to try to force *Campos de Níjar* into a straitjacket of one genre or another, for then it will always fall short: it is easy to object that there is too much socio-political protest in it for a travelogue, or that there is too much space taken up with aesthetically pleasing landscape description for a hard-hitting polemical documentary. But why should it have to be either one type of work or another? Let us rather assess it on its own merits as a text and nothing more restricting than that. Then we may find it an asset that it never becomes tedious through lack of variation, that just when one might begin to tire of landscape, here is a conversation and just when the misery of the locals' lives begins to become unbearably depressing, here is a beautiful view or a narrative section or a piece of interesting information about the region's customs or history. Thus, the different elements of the text may exist alongside one another and even heighten each other's effect through the contrast and refreshment they offer the reader; only if the work is judged narrowly by the yardstick of one genre or another will the varied nature of its composition seem detrimental. And since each of the different components of the text is accomplished so masterfully, as this Critical Guide has sought to demonstrate, and since they are blended so skilfully, one surely closes the book convinced that it is a masterpiece, small perhaps, modest perhaps, but a masterpiece nonetheless.

Bibliographical Note

1. Cano, José Luis, 'Juan Goytisolo: *Campos de Nijar*', *Insula*, no. 167 (1960), 8. A generally favourable review of the work, perhaps slightly dated in places.
2. Gil Casado, Pablo, *La novela social española (1920–1971)*, 2nd edn (Barcelona: Seix Barral, 1973). A general work, containing an interesting comparative study of a selection of travel texts from the period covered.
3. Goytisolo, Juan, 'Abandonemos de una vez el amoroso cultivo de nuestras señas de identidad', in his *Contracorrientes* (Barcelona: Montesinos, 1985), pp.134–38.
4. —, 'La Chanca, veinte años después', ibid., pp.162–66.
5. —, 'Volver al sur', ibid., pp.172–76.
6. Henn, David, 'Juan Goytisolo's Almería Travel Books and their Relationship to his Fiction', *Forum for Modern Language Studes*, 26 (1988), 256–71. Useful discussion, relating *Campos de Nijar* and *La Chanca* thematically to the Mendiola trilogy and touching on the first volume of the autobiography, *Coto vedado*.
7. Lázaro, Jesús, *La novelística de Juan Goytisolo* (Madrid: Alhambra, 1984). Only briefly touches on the travel works.
8. Lee Six, Abigail, *Juan Goytisolo: The Case for Chaos* (London: Yale University Press, 1990). A study that concentrates on the fiction from 1966 onwards, but deals briefly with earlier works including *Campos de Nijar* in Chapter 1.
9. Navajas, Gonzalo, *La novela de Juan Goytisolo*, Temas, 15 (Madrid: Sociedad General Española de Librería, 1979). Slightly more on the travel writings than in some of the other general works on Goytisolo.
10. Pérez, Genaro J., *Formalist Elements in the Novels of Juan Goytisolo* (Potomac, MD: Studia Humanitatis, 1979). Uses the terminology and approach of the Russian Formalist school of criticism, yet manages not to be obscure to the non-specialist reader.
11. Romero, Héctor R., *La evolución literaria de Juan Goytisolo* (Miami: Ediciones Universal, 1979). Mainly descriptive rather than analytical treatment of the travel works.
12. Sanz, Santos, *Lectura de Juan Goytisolo* (Barcelona: Víctor Pozanco, 1977). Negative (and not altogether justifiably so) view of *Campos de Nijar*.

13. Schaefer-Rodríguez, Claudia, 'Travel as a Rejection of History in the Works of Juan Goytisolo', *Revista Canadiense de Estudios Hispánicos*, 12 (1987–88), pp.159–68. Studies travel in Goytisolo's later fiction as well as in travel works themselves. Sees travel motif as escapist.

14. Schwartz, Kessel, *Juan Goytisolo*, Twayne World Authors Series, 104 (New York: Twayne, 1970). Mainly descriptive, somewhat simplistic on the whole, but better on *Campos de Níjar* than on most of the other texts studied.

15. Sobejano, Gonzalo, *Novela española de nuestro tiempo: en busca del pueblo perdido*, 2nd edn (Madrid: Prensa Española, 1975). General study, useful for placing *Campos de Níjar* in literary context.

16. Ugarte, Michael, *Trilogy of Treason: An Intertextual Study of Juan Goytisolo* (Columbia: University of Missouri Press, 1982). Devoted to Goytisolo's use of outside texts, mainly in later works, but briefly touching on *Campos de Níjar*, though more useful on *La Chanca*.

CRITICAL GUIDES TO SPANISH TEXTS

Edited by
J.E. Varey, A.D. Deyermond & C. Davies

CRITICAL GUIDES TO SPANISH TEXTS

Edited by
J.E. Varey, A.D. Deyermond & C. Davies